"Stuart Horwitz has done it again ... taining of his Book Architecture trilogy, ... _in Three Drafts_ is no less informative and packs ... instructional punch. With concrete steps to guide writers from that messy first draft to a polished manuscript, this book is a must-read for anyone who wants to get off the revision hamster wheel and finally get that book done."

"_Finish Your Book in Three Drafts_—a lofty promise, no? Veteran author and editor Stuart Horwitz delivers on his end. His process is much more comprehensive than a typical copy edit and the results are magical, judging by his own books and those of his highly successful clients."

"_Finish Your Book in Three Drafts_ will take the fear and confusion out of your book project by explaining the exact steps it takes to tackle a long narrative. You're never alone with this book in your hands. Horwitz explains how to begin, what to do next, and how to wrap it all up. Every writer should read this book before they begin a long project."

Hello Suzanne!
Thank you again for your support,
and I hope this engages with your
process!
all my best,
—S.

Finish Your Book in Three Drafts

HOW TO WRITE A BOOK,
REVISE A BOOK,
AND COMPLETE A BOOK
WHILE YOU STILL LOVE IT

WRITTEN BY
Stuart Horwitz

ILLUSTRATED BY
Dave Stebenne

For more information about this title, to book a workshop, or to hire a developmental editor trained in the Book Architecture Method, contact the publisher:

Book Architecture, LLC

One Richmond Square, Suite #112K

Providence, RI 02906

www.BookArchitecture.com

stuart@bookarchitecture.com

Twitter: @Book_Arch

Facebook: facebook.com/SeekTheMethod

ISBN: 978-0-9864204-2-9

Printed in the United States of America

CONTENTS:

CHAPTER FIVE:

The Method Draft, Part III: Finding Your Theme 83

Write That Method Draft! 95

CHAPTER SIX:

The Polished Draft, Part I: Role of the Beta Reader. 99

CHAPTER SEVEN:

The Polished Draft, Part II: Putting Together a Punch List 117

Write That Polished Draft! 124

CONCLUSION:

AUTHOR'S NOTE

This book incorporates nine videos and nine PDFs that are designed to enhance your reading experience. You can access these at the following web address: www.bookarchitecture.com/3d, by using the password: DRAFT.

Know What Draft You're In

I f you are thinking about writing a book, chances are that you are already a pretty good writer. Sure, we could all be better, but most of what we have to learn we will gain by practice and by reading books written by other people. Given that, this book is not about *how* to write, but rather about how to get yourself to the point where you are writing. And I think the best way to talk about the writing process is to consider the concept of drafts.

Have you ever asked yourself while writing, "How many drafts is this going to take?" That may seem like a question that can't have an answer, but I would like to propose that it does. And that answer is three. Three drafts, provided that each draft is approached in the right spirit and we take the time we need between drafts.

What comes between drafts is the part you may not know about. Some writers assume that the difference between a first draft and a final draft is a few revisions and a solid copy edit. What I am talking about here is a process that is more comprehensive and requires more patience. But the work pays off in robust benefits from each revision—each re-vision of the whole.

My goal is to give you the confidence that you are working on what you should be working on, that your efforts are focused, and that your time is well spent. It probably already makes intuitive sense to you that you can't work on more than one draft at a time. In this book, we will look at some mantras for each of the three drafts. Here's one for the process as a whole:

Know what draft you're in.

Each draft plays by different rules, and knowing what draft you're in can help you avoid writer's block. The first draft, for example, is meant to be written much more freely than is the third draft, which requires greater concentration of effort. Say you discover a hole in your story during the drafting process. You need to write that scene from scratch; therefore, even though you may be in the third draft, for that piece you need to play by first-draft rules. Otherwise, you will demand of it immediately a nuance and a measure that it cannot possibly achieve.

We will name each draft and detail the work that occurs between the first draft and second draft and between the second draft and third draft. But first, have I convinced you yet that your work will require three drafts, not one or twenty?

If you're a fan of the single draft idea, you might be remembering the stories of reporters bragging they could write newspaper articles by feeding paper into the back of the typewriter—when it came out the front, it was done. It may be possible to write a sentence like that: exactly as you want it to be for all time. But that's not how we approach excellence for a book-length work.

There is a literary myth that Jack Kerouac wrote *On the Road* in one draft, one Benzedrine- and marijuana-fueled draft, over a twenty-one-day period. It is true that he created a 120-foot roll of paper so that he wouldn't have to stop to feed more paper into his typewriter, and wrote one of his drafts that way. But it turns out that he was working from a draft he already had in his journals. Also, if you look at that typewriter scroll closely, you can see all kinds of corrections; those corrections are, in effect, his third draft.

Three drafts, not one. Also: three drafts, not forty-nine. You may have heard this cute story about Oscar Wilde: His host asked him how his writing was going, and he said, "I was working on the proof of one of my poems all the morning and took out a comma." "And in the afternoon?" "In the afternoon—well, I put it back in again."[1] That doesn't count as a draft. What you are trying to do is tackle your book, not tinker with it. Because—are you ready?—the point is not to go through life writing the same book the whole time.

We'll call the first draft the *messy draft*, which is all about getting it down. We'll call the second draft the *method draft*, which is all about making sense. And we'll call the third draft the *polished draft*, which is all about making it good. We could also call the third draft the *design draft* if you are publishing independently or the *agent draft* if you are seeking traditional publication. At least once a year, writers will approach me at a conference and tell me that they found the top ten agents in their genre and sent them their first draft (not their third draft) and now they are wishing they could turn back time.

· · · · · · · · · · · ·

1   Robert Harborough Sherard, *Oscar Wilde: The Story of an Unhappy Friendship* (London: Greening & Company, Ltd., 1905), 72.

I want to save you that heartache. To do so, I will perhaps exaggerate the differences among the drafts in order to simplify matters for our use. Also to keep things simple, when we get into an area which could get pretty intense, I will continue the discussion in a PDF posted on my website. (The code to unlock these nine PDFs is provided in the front of this book.) These PDFs contain more detailed information and instructions, which is why they are labeled "Going Deeper." That way, while you're reading this book, you can choose how in-depth you want to go in the moment and what you might want to go back to later.

Sometimes I will refer to material found in one of my first two books: *Blueprint Your Bestseller* (hereafter, *BYB*) and *Book Architecture* (*BA*). I will try to keep those references to a minimum, and you certainly don't have to read those books to understand what I'm saying in this one.

Finally, this book incorporates nine videos that are designed to enhance your reading experience. You can access these on the same website where the PDFs are located (bookarchitecture.com/3d). They are short, with an average run time of less than a minute and a half. I would bring you popcorn if I could. I won't guilt you into watching them by describing *all the trouble* we went to in making these videos for you—instead, for each video, we have included here a storyboard version with the complete script. I'll just say that if you do watch them, remember what appeared at the beginning of Martin Scorsese's film *The Last Waltz*, about The Band's final concert on Thanksgiving Day in 1976: THIS FILM SHOULD BE PLAYED LOUD.

There is a reason that we are switching the medium here and engaging with these short films, in addition to whatever entertainment value they might provide. When you start talking about process and revision and structure, it can get very abstract if we don't have at least one example in common. I could say, "Remember, in *The Matrix*, when…" and some people may not have seen that movie. Or I could say, "Remember, in *East of Eden*, when…" but you may not have read that book.

*AS AN EXAMPLE, I HAVEN'T SEEN THAT MOVIE OR READ THAT BOOK.

In conclusion, let's suck the fear out of the book-writing process. We can all do three drafts. Everything you will read about in here—how to generate material, how to find your theme, how to use beta readers, etc.—can all take place at the proper time, and you can get a great book on the page.

I'm looking forward to our time together.

"Now, practically even better news than that of short assignments is the idea of shitty first drafts. All good writers write them. This is how they end up with good second drafts and terrific third drafts."

— ANNE LAMOTT

CHAPTER ONE

The Messy Draft: How to Generate Material

Thank you, Anne Lamott, for corroborating (on the previous page) the three-draft process right off the bat. I mentioned earlier that we would be calling the first draft the messy draft, tempting as it may be to call it the shitty draft. How do you feel about writing something messy? If that notion gives you a shiver, you may be, by nature, more of an *outliner* than a *pantser*.

You may have heard that there is this debate about who has a better way to write between pantsers and outliners. A pantser is someone who, as the name suggests, writes by the seat of his or her pants. An outliner, on the other hand, is someone who meticulously crafts every writing session.

This isn't a real debate, by the way, because we are all both of these at different times. Even the most ardent pantsers are bound to somehow keep track of where they are going next and what they have already accomplished, while even the most rigorous outliners get surprised when they sit at their desks and discover something about their books that they didn't already know. There's an interplay between outlining and pantsing, and while every writer is different, I suggest that you create the messy draft by pantsing.

"And in this corner!..." It kind of looks like a boxing ad, doesn't it? In the left corner, we have Biz, your prototypical pantser. And in the other corner, we see Ro$hi, who has an outlining system that he wants to impart. Rather than identifying exclusively with one or the other, I think it is helpful to think of these two characters as different sides of one's own psyche. Then we can see what happens when they interact.

We start with Biz, a fellow writer whose experience may mirror your own, as she boards her pencil train and continues her journey as a writer.

[Watch Video One: Biz on the Train]

...I WROTE MOST OF MY BOOK IN 5 MONTHS.

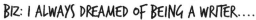

BIZ: I ALWAYS DREAMED OF BEING A WRITER....

IT JUST FLOWED, I DON'T KNOW. I COULDN'T WAIT TO GET HOME AND WORK ON IT.

WRITING IS SO MUCH FUN! BUT I NEVER KNEW HOW MUCH WORK IT WOULD BE.

AND THEN I HAD NO IDEA WHAT TO DO.

I MOVED SOME PARAGRAPHS AROUND.

I TRIED TO PUT THE MIDDLE AT THE BEGINNING
TO MAKE IT MORE INTERESTING.

IT STOPPED BEING FUN.

IT WAS EXHAUSTING.

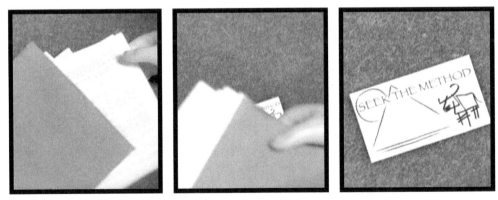

WHEN I GOT HOME FROM WORK, I HAD BETTER THINGS TO DO.

Now, I know what some of you may be thinking: "That sheaf of papers that Biz is holding...I don't even have that much material yet." So let's back up. In my first book, *BYB*, I wrote a chapter titled "How to Generate Material" and called it Action Step Zero. As in, start here. I'll try not to repeat myself too much, but everyone has his or her own favorite tricks or tips, and these are still my six favorites.

#1. Count Your Words

It seems so anal-retentive, I know, but I count my words for every writing session regardless of what draft I'm in. The computer makes it easy: You can highlight the new section and get the word count in five seconds. But I count even if I'm writing longhand, which I still do sometimes.

Do you ever switch up the medium that you use to write? I recommend it; I wrote the first draft, the messy draft, of this book on my great-uncle's refurbished Hermes 3000 typewriter from the 1960s. I found that doing so removed some of the pressure that I was feeling to get every concept right—I mean, no one is going to read this, with the typewritten xxxxxxxxxx through the places where I was temporarily blocked and the handwritten squiggles that indicated the reordering of ideas, right?

We count our words, because you cannot simultaneously create and know the value of what you are creating—it is like looking in two directions at once. In exchange for quality, then, we go with quantity.

Do you know how many words you typically write during a good session? That is a good thing to be aware of, because then you can set a goal of how many words you want to write in a month. You may have done NaNoWriMo (National Novel Writing Month), an annual novel-writing project in which participants are encouraged to write 50,000 words during the month of November. That is one pantsing thrill ride. And it may not be necessary. Even if you write only 10,000 words in a month, you can still be Biz's equal when she says, "I wrote most of my book in five months!" In *BYB*, I recommended exactly that: producing 10,000 words a month; I called it the 10K challenge. But to get there, you have to count your words.

MINE IS 1,752, BUT I'LL GLADLY TAKE 1,000.

#2. Find a Neutral Audience

I don't know about you, but when I write I find myself avoiding the critics in my mind—those people who bring harsh or careless energy—and seeking out the cheerleaders—those people who I know have my back. But that doesn't really get it in the end. Those critics and cheerleaders are kind of two sides of the same tortured psychic coin.

It's better to find a neutral voice to write to. On the next page, we see Ro$hi, whose neutrality is symbolized by his blank book face. While the critics may say, "You're working in a pretty crowded field..." and the cheerleaders may say, "I've never heard anything like your story..." the neutral audience member just says, if it's fiction, "What happens next?"

and if it's nonfiction, "What do I need to know about this?" It's kind of the corollary to the idea that, if you don't know whether what you're writing is any good, why not write to someone else who doesn't know either?

The cheerleader and the critic will appear later in this book in a rather frightening nightmare that Biz has. Neither are very useful, and I try to stress this when I teach a class as well; there are two things you can't say about someone else's manuscript. You can't say, "I love it." And you can't say, "I guess I'm just not your audience" (which is code for "I hate it"). You have to try to be a neutral audience.

Before we leave the second tip, let's reflect on the concept of *audience*, now that we have handled the concept of *neutral*. In your mind, you want to write to someone, or a small group of people, who will actually read your book. Some of them could become your beta readers, who we will discuss in chapter six. If you are writing a book about meditation and running, you will want to picture someone ideally who meditates and runs. You might also picture someone who either meditates or runs, thinking that you might convince him or her to try the other activity. But I wouldn't pick someone who scoffs at the over-examined life and doesn't like to get off the couch. Unless you really are that good.

#3. Don't Try to Organize Anything

This tip drives outliners crazy. Sometimes clients come to me with these complex notes before they've ever written a word, and I have to tell them that's kinda not the way it works. It could work that way if you were writing a reportorial nonfiction account, and your notes comprise the outline of true events.

But for the rest of us, I think it's like E.M. Forster said: "How can I know what I think until I see what I say?" Meaning, things need to get messy.

Pantsing, remember? I have heard that writers need permission to generate material in this way, probably from the outliner side of them, which likes to make plans but can't bring itself to start. It also helps if you trust that there will be a method for fishing out the repetitions and for strengthening the foundations between the first draft and the second draft. That is what the method draft section of this book is all about.

This tip, by the way, is particularly hard for perfectionists to employ. If I am coaching a perfectionist, I will usually try to humor them. "Yes, indeed! I agree with you, by all means, let's write a perfect first draft. Now, how do we do that?..."

Does a perfect first draft strangle opportunities before they have a chance to breathe? Okay, that may be a leading question. Think of what a first draft is for a sculptor, say, Michelangelo, who is excavating a rough-hewn block of marble from a quarry. He's not going to stare at it and ask, "Why aren't you the Pietà yet?"

A perfect first draft covers the ground. A perfect first draft tries material out. A perfect first draft makes a start in a lot of places. A perfect first draft familiarizes you with your material—or, at least, the portion of it that is available to your conscious mind. Successive drafts will fill that reservoir further, deepen your understanding of what you are doing, and enable you to tighten connections and layer in nuances.

Everybody's different; some very smart people I know rewrite the same chapter over and over again before moving on. Sometimes this causes them to advance very slowly, which can lead to a crisis of confidence ("Why aren't we further along than this by now?"). They tell me that they are doing this because they are seeking coherence. I gently remind them that coherence will be possible only when we get to the end of the messy draft and look back to see, "What are we trying to make cohere?" That work leads to the second draft, what we call the method draft.

In sum, disorganization is an excellent sign. It means that you haven't picked a subject that is too easy and your conclusions aren't too pat. You are allowing the drafting process to accomplish something big and organic. Keep writing the first draft, and keep being okay when it feels like a mess.

#4. Make the Time

This one is pretty obvious. These are all pretty obvious actually, but there are a lot of aspiring writers who aren't doing this currently. If you want, you can email me, and we can compare notes on day jobs, out-of-town guests, aging parents, child care, grueling commutes, and so forth. The point is, that we make time for these responsibilities, so why don't we make time for writing?

This is Biz going to a coffee shop in a universe parallel to Portland, Oregon. Biz is going to make the time. Let's say that she has allotted two hours for herself to write today. That means she is going to park the car, run into the bank to get quarters to feed the meter, order her one-pump-mocha-one-pump-vanilla-nonfat-latte-for-the-win, sit down, and then her two hours starts. After two full hours, then she'll get up to do whatever she does in her stop-motion action world.

Nobody is going to make the time for Biz. If she tells other people that she is a writer, chances are that the first question they will ask her is "Are you published?" In Western society, we are all supposed to be producing things, all the time. If your books are for sale and are selling well, you're all right; otherwise, you should be hand-sewing the kids' Halloween costumes, or out on the boat with the rest of your friends, or finding a job at which you can work more hours.

Making time to generate material—disorganized material, at that!—is not looked upon very warmly, even if you do tell people your word count. They would rather you tell them you were going golfing, or back to church for the second time that same day, than that you were going to write. Maybe they are secretly afraid they are in your book.

Whatever the case, the journey for Biz to call herself a writer, and to announce that to whomever is in her life, is hers to take alone. Everything takes effort, and to follow this path in particular requires solitary discipline. The way I look at it, everybody who makes time for their writing can call themselves a writer.

Two quick points: First, when you are scheduling your writing sessions, schedule an extra one each week so that when "life" gets in the way you can let that day go, like a baseball game getting rained out. If you find yourself skipping more than one session per week, life isn't getting in your way…you are. Second, if you see writers in a coffee shop—don't talk to them. You're an extra in their movie.

#5. Listen

So then the question comes up, "Should I count my hours?" And the answer is no. We're going to count our words and make the time. If you write, say, a thousand words per day, you know that you need to have ten writing sessions during the month to total the 10,000 words that I recommended in the first tip, "Count Your Words." But we're not going to start counting the minutes, outside of scheduling enough time for today's writing session. The reason is that when you make the time and you get your ego out of the way—easier said than done—your words flow at a certain pace.

Saul Bellow called it the *prompter*, that voice inside your inner ear that spools out your writing to you just before you think it up consciously.[2] He said that each of us has one. That prompter proceeds at its own pace. When we count our words, we get a sense of what a good session hanging out with our prompter will yield.

· · · · · · · · · · ·

2 Saul Bellow, "The Art of Fiction," *Paris Review* 36 (Winter 1966): 57.

The prompter is what we are listening for, as the name of this tip indicates. Or, if you prefer, we are listening to our "voice." I think people make a lot out of the literary concept of voice, especially when it comes to discovering one's voice. Your voice is simply the voice you hear in your head, when you remove all of the other distractions.

How do you remove distractions from your life? You might exercise, or meditate, or consume adult beverages, or do some combination of activities that add up to your personal ritual. It is trial and error, but that doesn't make it impossible. Whatever your ritual, it should have two things going for it: It should open you up, so that you can listen, and it should strengthen you, so that you are not afraid of what you hear.

#6. Have Fun

This is the last, and most important, way to generate material. I'm not talking about stupid fun. I'm talking about being alive in the moment, being curious because you don't know what's going to happen next. Enjoyment: That is the whole idea of pantsing.

Now, pantsing doesn't have to be as extreme as it seems. You might show up for your first-draft writing session with a few scribbled bullet points to keep by your side; I'm not suggesting that you stare at a blank screen with nothing to give you a push. But just like you don't want to start with nothing, you also don't want to start with too much. Here's another mantra:

The notes you have taken are not as
important as the place you are in.

Besides, if you have made the time in this culture that isn't falling all over aspiring writers, shouldn't you at least enjoy yourself?

This is me having fun.

This is the filmmaker, Dave Stebenne, having fun. Someone said that you shouldn't show the behind-the-scenes stuff...but I think the point is that everything is made somehow, and if you can retain the excitement you felt when you were first discovering your material—this is the White Ox, who we are going to meet in a minute—then I think that energy can be preserved in the final product as a kind of joy.

As we come to the end of the messy draft, I would like to offer you one final mantra for this part of the process:

Keep it moving

You may remember the story of Lot's wife in Genesis 19 in the Bible. Reportedly, she turned into a pillar of salt when she turned back to look at the destruction of the city of Sodom. I'm not going to comment on the believability of that event, but this is how I see writers who try to edit their work the next day and the day after that.

What is there to see back there, exactly? What you screwed up? It will still be there, believe me. But at the same time, it will change. Rainier Maria Rilke once advised a young poet to "Live the questions now. Perhaps then, someday far in the future, you will gradually, without even noticing it, live your way into the answer."[3] We don't have until someday far in the future, but we do have a three-draft process during which we can let things play out.

· · · · · · · · · · · ·

3 Rainer Maria Rilke, *Letters to a Young Poet* (New York: W.W. Norton, 1993), 13.

Write That Messy Draft!

If you haven't written your messy draft, the time has come. Just get it down; give yourself something to work with. You can't mess up the messy draft. It is also important to note that first drafts usually don't end, in the conventional sense. Sometimes a client will tell me, "Well, I wrote 79,000 words, but I didn't finish it." I say, hey—if you wrote nearly eighty thousand words, you finished your first draft—even if you didn't type "The End." You may not have finished your third draft, but that's what the three-draft process is for.

If you've already written a messy draft—or an advanced draft, for that matter—that's okay. We'll just call the draft you are in now the first draft. (Sorry about that.) You can read the title of this book as "Finish Your Book in Two More Drafts."

Here are a few more mantras to keep you company while you write your messy draft:

* *try it out*
* *go on*
* *cover the ground*
* *believe in yourself (first)*
* *propose it*
* *get the feel*
* *put it in*
* *assemble your materials*

* *lose the sense of rush*
* *take the brakes off*
* *smile; that's where it all happens*
* *make a start*
* *write long*
* *let it come*
* *find your stride*

"The idea is the whole thing. If you stay true to the idea, it tells you everything you need to know, really. You just keep working to make it look like that idea looked, feel like it felt, sound like it sounded, and be the way it was... It's an intuition: You feel-think your way through. You start one place, and as you go, it gets more and more finely tuned. But all along it's the idea talking. At some point, it feels correct to you. And you hope that it feels somewhat correct to others."

— DAVID LYNCH

CHAPTER TWO:

Seek the Method

Earlier I said that a work could be completed in three drafts, provided that each draft is approached in the right spirit and we take the time we need between drafts to benefit each revision. But writers often don't want to pause between drafts. They are feeling the mojo. If they stop, they might not be able to recapture that mysterious groove they have going. And they certainly don't want to pause to analyze their own work, because then it might lose its life, as if all analysis were over-analysis.

But that is exactly what the second draft—the method draft—requires. We might need permission to begin, permission to write a slew of messy pages, but we also need permission to stop. Now that the messy draft is done, we must stop the wheels from spinning, or we will dig ourselves a hopelessly deep rut.

Intelligent Planning is Not the Enemy of Creative Genius

In my experience, the *longer* the period you can wait between drafts, the better. Your eyes will be fresher, and you will be able to edit harder and more effectively. This is helpful, because if the messy draft was about getting it down, the method draft is about making sense. "Intelligent planning is not the enemy of creative genius," as we like to say around the office. We don't actually say that, but it is hung on the wall.

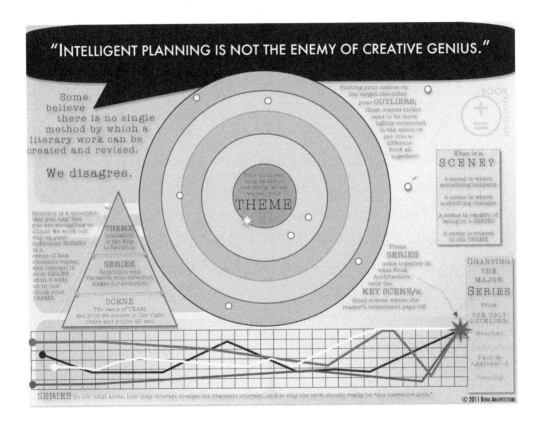

By intelligent planning, I am referring to embracing the part of you that is an outliner. The method draft is to outlining as the messy draft was to pantsing. I have heard some pantsers refer to outlining as their Kryptonite. That's a pretty strong statement, but I think I understand where that nervous apprehension comes from. For pantsers, it is writing from scratch that brings the purest joy. After that, they may recognize the efficacy of getting—and staying—organized, but that is paired with the instinctual fear that their favorite part of the process is behind them.

As we prepare to write the method draft, my aim is to promote that joy of discovery all the way through by expanding our view of what being creative means. Sometimes creativity is the perfect sentence; sometimes creativity is knowing where that sentence goes and what comes before it and after it. Sometimes you get ideas for the structure of what you are writing, sometimes you get ideas about the content of what you are writing. Both are immensely valuable, and if we allow creativity to encompass the whole, then much of the process can be positively unexpected. When that stops, I agree, we should stop; that is why I am trying to get you through this process in three drafts, and not twenty.

By outline, here I am referring to any class of graphs, lists, or diagrams—or, if you are familiar with my work, grids, targets, and arcs. You can think of outlining, at this point, as creating a map of a territory you are just discovering; just because you know the soundings of where you can land a boat, that doesn't mean you know the interior geography of the country. When something is mapped out completely, it may lose its mystique, but I don't think you run the risk of that just between a first draft and a second draft.

Writer's Block

Some pantsers still won't listen to me. They will just keep writing, revising as they go, and adding new parts, and doubting some of their changes, and eventually many of them will get stuck entirely.

That's what happened to Biz. And then this happens:

[Watch Video Two: Biz Meets the White Ox]

BIZ: AM I LIKE...
SUPPOSED TO ASK
YOU SOMETHING?

OX: YOU SEEK THE METHOD.

BIZ: OH GREAT. A TALKING OX.

MOOOOO!...

I'm not really sure how this kind of thing happens. Let's blame the filmmaker, Dave, shall we? You start working with other people, and they have skill sets that you don't have, and before you know it you have a White Ox in your book. Collaboration takes you in directions you don't expect... Speaking of directions, the White Ox seems to be pointing in a direction. But where are we going?

Biz is based on a real person, and I stole the image above from her Facebook page. In *BYB*, I compared the drafting process to a mountain trek in which organization was represented by the upward climb and revision by the descent afterward. But that was just a diagram in black and white. What if we really headed out toward the metaphorical mountain of organization and revision?

[Watch Video Three: Biz's Mountain Journey]

BIZ: I SHOULD'VE STAYED IN BROOKLYN... .

OF COURSE. THE WHITE OX
DOESN'T, LIKE, STOP AND
WAIT FOR BIZ.

TWITTER ISN'T EVEN WORKING.

CAN'T I GET AIRLIFTED?
IN A HELICOPTER?

BIZ: SO, THIS IS THE PART, WHERE SOMEBODY TELLS ME IT'S ABOUT THE JOURNEY AND NOT THE DESTINATION, RIGHT?

So that's Ro$hi, who we met earlier. And that's the cave where he lives. And that's called the "willing suspension of disbelief," for those of you familiar with that quote by the poet Samuel Coleridge.[4]

But Biz's disbelief isn't all that willing:

· · · · · · · · · · ·

4 The full quote runs, "(Our) endeavours should be directed to...transfer from our inward nature a human interest and a semblance of truth sufficient to procure for these shadows of imagination that willing suspension of disbelief for the moment, which constitutes poetic faith." Samuel Coleridge, *The Major Works* (Oxford: Oxford University Press, 2009), 314.

[Watch Video Four: Biz and Ro$hi Fight]

BIZ: MY BOOK IS A MESS!   RO$HI: THERE IS A METHOD.

BIZ: WHAT HAVE I LEFT OUT? HOW DO I END IT? WHERE ARE ALL THESE SUBPLOTS GOING? WHAT AM I EVEN WRITING ABOUT? SHOULD I STOP?

RO$HI: LOOK TO THE ANCIENT ART OF REVISION.

BIZ: BUT MY MFA TEACHER SAYS—

RO$HI: THERE IS A METHOD.

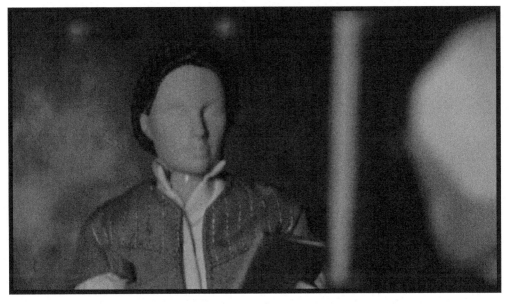

BIZ: BUT MY MOM SAYS—   RO$HI: THERE IS A METHOD.

BIZ: YOU DON'T KNOW ANYTHING ABOUT MY BOOK. WHAT ARE YOU PUSHING?
SOME KIND OF FORMULA?

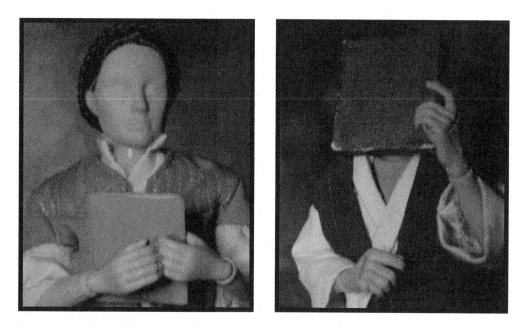

RO$HI: YOUR EARS DO NOT HEAR. THIS IS A METHOD, NOT A FORMULA.

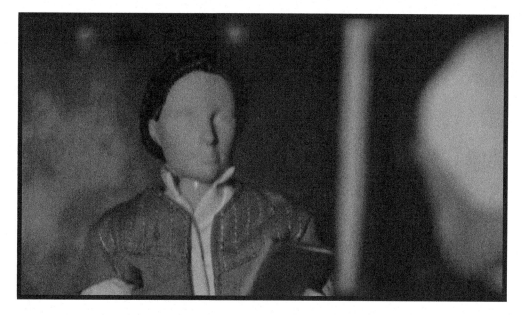

BIZ: THE ANCIENT ART OF REVISION? CHILL MR. MIYAGI, THIS IS NOT THE KARATE KID. YOU CAN'T WRITE A GOOD BOOK WITH A METHOD.

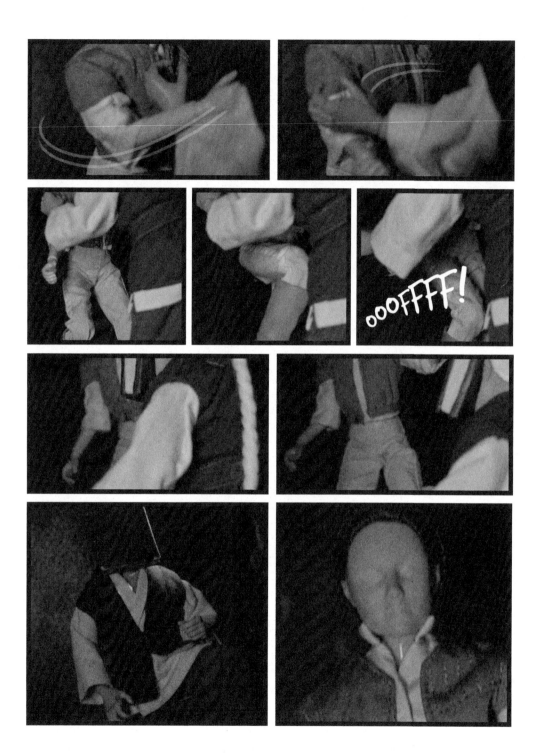

As I mentioned in the introduction of this book, there is a reason we are engaging with these characters. This way we will have a common example when we start getting more technical, doing things such as defining scenes and working with scenes. The first two definitions of scene I like to use are: 1) A scene is where something happens and 2) A scene is where because something happens, something changes. In this case, what changes after Biz and Ro$hi fight is their dynamic: Ro$hi has increased respect for Biz, and Biz becomes willing to listen to Ro$hi...at least for a little while.

> GOING DEEPER: *PDF #1: The Five Definitions of Scene. This PDF discusses all five definitions of scene (the first two of which are mentioned here) and how they relate to each other.*

[Watch Video Five: The First Draft Is the Easy Part]

RO$HI: THE FIRST DRAFT IS THE EASY PART.

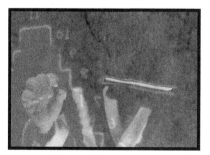

THE BOOK ARCHITECTURE METHOD IS A 22–STEP PROCESS FOR ORGANIZING AND REVISING YOUR MANUSCRIPT.

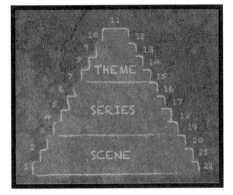

IT HAS HELPED BESTSELLING AUTHORS GET FROM FIRST DRAFT TO FINAL DRAFT.

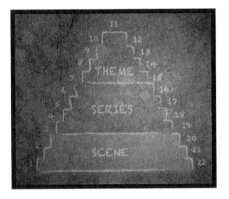

22 MAY SEEM LIKE A BIG NUMBER. REALLY THE NUMBER YOU NEED TO KNOW IS THREE; SCENE...

...SERIES...

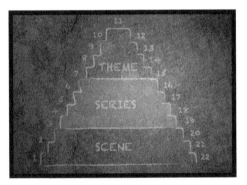

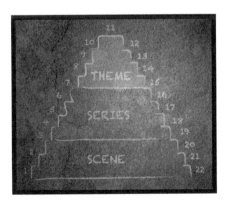

...AND THEME.

The First Draft Is the Easy Part

A few notes: The first draft isn't really the easy part. It's just the one that's behind us now, so maybe Ro$hi is using that as motivation. As he just mentioned, the Book Architecture Method has twenty-two steps, which are described in *BYB*. You might use some of them, or all of them, or none of them. In the following three chapters on preparing for the method draft, I introduce eight action steps: brainstorming your scenes; identifying your good, bad, forgotten, and missing scenes; cutting up your scenes; making a series grid; and using the theme target. You can use my method. Or you can use somebody else's method. Or, even better, you can create your own method out of everything you read and everything you try that works for you.

CHAPTER THREE

The Method Draft, Part I: Working with Scenes

I n the previous video, Ro$hi mentioned the three core concepts of the Book Architecture Method: scene, series, and theme. Each of the next three chapters will focus on preparing the second draft, the method draft, through each of these three lenses in sequence, beginning with scene.

Let's look at some action steps that relate to scene.

Brainstorm Your Scenes

The first thing I generally recommend is to brainstorm a list of your scenes. Give each scene a name, something that takes you back there in your mind. If you're writing fiction, you might consider a scene a unified action happening in a certain place at a certain time. If you are writing nonfiction, you can consider a scene any discrete batch of information that can be placed under a subhead. The important thing is to get used to what a scene is for you. After studying your own work, you might realize: "I tend to start scenes this way, I tend to conclude them in a certain way, and so forth."

The only catch is: You can't look at the book itself.

Why don't we look at the manuscript? Because the memory is the surest guide to the memorable. If we forget a scene, it isn't strike three. But it is strike one, and should be treated as such. People say, "I'll remember every scene in my book," but in fifteen years of working with clients and students I have never come across one who could.

Here is a partial list of Biz's scenes. By the way, Biz is a very good writer even though sometimes she lacks confidence. She is writing a memoir, so her work straddles the line between non-fiction (she claims that this stuff really happened) and fiction (she wants to use some techniques for rearranging the order of her material). Her book doesn't have a title yet. She describes it as being about "waiting for this part of my life to be over and figuring out if I want to have children."

- THIS APARTMENT WAS SUPPOSED TO FIX MY LIFE
- THE ABSOLUTE WORST HUMAN TO LIVE WITH
- AWKWARD PIZZA PARTY
- THE SCORPIONS WILL EAT YOUR FEET
- FOOD – THE FOUNDATION OF SELF-CARE (OR SELF-NEGLECT)
- MY OFFICE WAS THE OFFICE BEFORE THE OFFICE WAS THE OFFICE
- WHEN DO WE START YELLING IN THE STREET

Biz's Good Scenes

- THIS APARTMENT WAS SUPPOSED TO FIX MY LIFE
- THE ABSOLUTE WORST HUMAN TO LIVE WITH
- AWKWARD PIZZA PARTY
- THE SCORPIONS WILL EAT YOUR FEET
- FOOD – THE FOUNDATION OF SELF-CARE (OR SELF-NEGLECT)
- MY OFFICE WAS THE OFFICE BEFORE THE OFFICE WAS THE OFFICE
- WHEN DO WE START YELLING IN THE STREET

Biz's next step is to go through her list of scenes and highlight the "good" ones in green.

By good, I mean good enough. By good, I mean done for now. If you had to let somebody read a scene from your work in progress, you might choose one of these scenes. We don't want to lack self-esteem to the point where we are afraid to label anything as good. That leads directly to writing the same book for the rest of your life. Instead, we want to figure out which parts to work on when we revise, and we do this in part by figuring out what we don't have to work on (much). We can't work on everything at the same time, or it'll be like we are chasing our tails, and the whole thing devolves into chaos.

Biz's Bad Scenes

Besides, we have work to do. Next, Biz is going to go through her scene list and highlight the "bad" ones in pink. By bad, I don't mean morally bad, obviously. I mean the scenes that you didn't nail. They cause you some anxiety, because you are pretty sure they need to be in your book but in their current state they make you think *maybe I should just chuck this whole writing thing.*

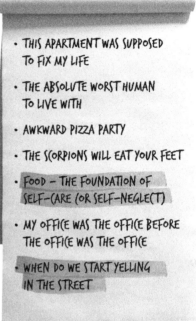

- THIS APARTMENT WAS SUPPOSED TO FIX MY LIFE
- THE ABSOLUTE WORST HUMAN TO LIVE WITH
- AWKWARD PIZZA PARTY
- THE SCORPIONS WILL EAT YOUR FEET
- FOOD – THE FOUNDATION OF SELF-CARE (OR SELF-NEGLECT)
- MY OFFICE WAS THE OFFICE BEFORE THE OFFICE WAS THE OFFICE
- WHEN DO WE START YELLING IN THE STREET

So why are these bad scenes?

Biz may have identified "Food-the Foundation of Self-Care or Self Neglect" as a bad scene because nothing happens. Remember, if nothing happens, nothing changes, and it's not a scene. What about this scene?

The scene "When Do We Start Yelling in the Street" might be bad because she's too attached to it. A bad scene is like a bad relationship, you have to figure it out, solve it, before you move on. Anyone?

Biz's Forgotten Scenes

We still haven't gone back to the manuscript. Now is the time to do that. Here is a small sampling of the scenes that Biz forgot (because she did not remember all of them):

Why did Biz forget these scenes? She may have forgotten "Roommate Etiquette 101," because it is a paler version of "The Absolute Worst Human to Live With." If she was heeding the messy draft tip "Don't Try to Organize Anything," it is quite likely she would have ended up with several versions of a scene trying to do the same thing. In preparation for the method draft, she can locate these multiple versions so that in the method draft she can replace them with one uberscene that incorporates the best parts of all of them.

I have no idea why she forgot the scene, "Free Will Used to Be a Friend of Mine." I think maybe this would have been better as a bumper sticker.

Biz's Missing Scenes

There is a fourth kind of scene that we call missing. Missing scenes are simply scenes that you haven't written yet. You want to keep your scene list going the whole time, and you can add your missing scenes to the bottom and highlight them in orange, as Biz is doing here.

- AWKWARD PIZZA PARTY
- THE SCORPIONS WILL EAT YOUR FEET
- FOOD – THE FOUNDATION OF SELF-CARE (OR SELF-NEGLECT)
- MY OFFICE WAS THE OFFICE BEFORE THE OFFICE WAS THE OFFICE
- WHEN DO WE START YELLING IN THE STREET
- ROOMMATE ETIQUETTE 101
- FREE WILL USED TO BE A FRIEND OF MINE

- THIS APARTMENT WAS SUPPOSED TO FIX MY LIFE
- THE ABSOLUTE WORST HUMAN TO LIVE WITH
- AWKWARD PIZZA PARTY
- THE SCORPIONS WILL EAT YOUR FEET
- FOOD – THE FOUNDATION OF SELF-CARE (OR SELF-NEGLECT)
- ROOMMATE ETIQUETTE 101

You come across the need for one, or you come up with the bright idea for one, so you add its name to this list. We have to remember, though, that the first time we write a missing scene, that will be a first draft of it, and so we have to play by first-draft rules. If we try to write a missing scene from scratch and make it stand up to the standards of a more advanced draft, well, we are sure to run our pencil train into the concrete barrier of writer's block.

- MY OFFICE WAS THE OFFICE BEFORE THE OFFICE WAS THE OFFICE
- FOOD – THE FOUNDATION OF SELF-CARE (OR SELF-NEGLECT)
- ROOMMATE ETIQUETTE 101
- FREE WILL USED TO BE A FRIEND OF MINE
- A GENTLE DISCUSSION ABOUT MY CRAZY ULTIMATUMS
- GRATEFUL FOR THE COSMIC SCAVENGER HUNT
- THE STUFF MY MOM WOULD ORCHESTRATE AN HONOR KILLING FOR

As I mentioned, Biz is based on a real person, and originally she stipulated that I could use this last example of a missing scene ("The Stuff My Mom Would Orchestrate an Honor Killing For") only when I was presenting my work west of the Mississippi. I don't know where you are reading this book, so *sshhh...* (I don't even see why it's so bad, it isn't like it says what an honor killing would have to be orchestrated for...)

Cut Up Your Scenes

So, there are four kinds of scenes: good, bad, forgotten, and missing. And now comes the fun part: We cut them up!

[Watch Video Six: Cut Up Your Scenes]

BIZ: YOU WANT ME TO WHAT?

RO$HI: I WANT YOU TO FIND THE PLACES WHERE THE SCENES BREAK, AND I WANT YOU TO CUT YOUR MANUSCRIPT INTO ALL OF ITS INDEPENDENT SCENES.

BIZ: UM, FIRST OF ALL, I USE SCRIVENER FOR THAT. I'M NOT IN KINDERGARTEN. WHAT NEXT, GLUE STICKS AND GLITTER?

RO$HI: ACTUALLY, I USE A STAPLER.

RO$HI: WHEN YOU USE THE COMPUTER, IT'S TOO EASY TO SAY "I'M HAVING AN OFF DAY," AND JUST REVERT TO AN OLDER VERSION OF THE MANUSCRIPT. I RECOMMEND AT LEAST ONCE PER PROJECT, YOU CUT IT UP...

BIZ: AGHHH! WHAT ARE YOU DOING?

RO$HI: …YOU KNOW, BLESS THE TREE THAT WANTS TO BECOME A BOOK— WHAT'S THAT SAYING?

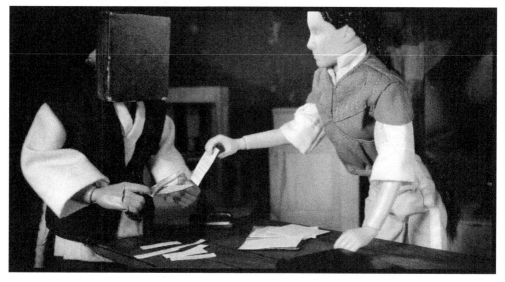

BIZ: "EVERY TREE ASPIRES TO BECOME A BOOK." GIVE ME THAT! YOU DON'T EVEN KNOW WHAT YOU'RE DOING.

RO$HI: AND THEN WE CAN SEE WHICH SCENES ARE MEATY AND WHICH SCENES YOU'VE JUST BEEN DRAGGING AROUND, DRAFT TO DRAFT,…

…THAT REALLY BELONG IN THIS PILE.

BIZ: THAT IS ABSOLUTELY TERRIFYING. WHAT IF, LIKE, THE
BEST LINE EVER WRITTEN BY A HUMAN BEING ENDS UP STUCK UNDER THAT PILE?

RO$HI: WE HAVE TO
SEE THE FOREST FOR
THE TREES.

BIZ: THE SAME TREES
WE CUT DOWN TO
MAKE ALL THESE
BOOKS?—

RO$HI: AND WE HAVE
TO MOVE ON.

BIZ: BUT DOES IT HAVE TO BE THIS COMPLICATED?

RO$HI: IF THE WAY PRESENTED TO YOU SEEMS EASY, IT IS PROBABLY FALSE.

BIZ: BUT WHAT IF SCENE 1 IS STILL SCENE 1?
AND SCENES 2 & 3 ARE STILL SCENES 2 & 3?

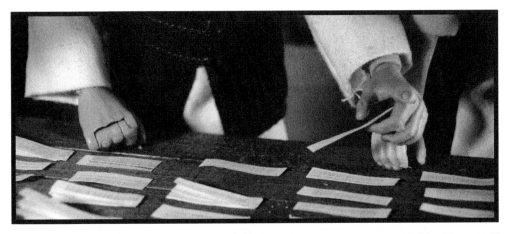

RO$HI: AND WHAT IF SCENE 4 IS ACTUALLY SCENE 17? WE BREAK YOUR MANUSCRIPT DOWN TO THE LEVEL OF UNIT BECAUSE UNIT + UNIT + UNIT = UNITY. AND THAT WAY WE CAN TAKE THE BEST PARTS UP A LEVEL.

BIZ: BUT HOW DID YOU DO THAT? HOW DO YOU KNOW THAT'S THE RIGHT ORDER? HOW DO YOU KNOW WHICH THE BEST PARTS ARE?

GOING DEEPER: *PDF #2: Cut Up Your Scenes. If you want to see the action step of cutting up your scenes described using real people and their manuscripts, this PDF is a visual and narrative description of working through this process with three clients.*

CHAPTER FOUR

The Method Draft, Part II: Discovering Your Series

W hat we saw at the end of the previous video looks great, right? (You did watch it, didn't you?) All those neatly arranged scenes ready for the next draft, which we are calling the method draft. I'll bet Biz feels confident that the order of her scenes is at least provisionally correct, that each scene will flow into the next, and that she can go deeper into the material, which is really what a second draft should be about.

But how do we get there? Ro$hi says, "Unit plus unit plus unit equals unity." That makes sense as far as working with individual scenes. But how, as Biz asks, can we be sure what the "best parts" are to take up a level? The answer to that question leads us to the second part of preparing for the method draft: discovering your series.

*BY SERIES, WE DO NOT MEAN A SET OF VOLUMES IN THE SAME GENRE AND THAT SHARE SOME CHARACTERS. NOT THAT ONE.

There is a lot that I could say about series. In fact, I wrote a whole book with series work as the premise, *Book Architecture*. I highly recommend it. I am going to steal that book's definition of series for our purpose here:

Series is the repetition and variation of a narrative element so that the repetition and variation creates meaning.

You may have heard *repetition and variation* applied to art in general: the use of melody in music, architectural patterns, and so forth. Repetition and variation *of a narrative element*—what is that? A narrative element is anything that can be identified by a reader as something discrete, for example, an object, a person, a place, a phrase, or a relationship. In fact, the repetitions and variations of series are how an object becomes a symbol, how a person becomes a character, how a place becomes a setting, how a repeated phrase becomes key to the philosophy of the work, and how a relationship becomes a dynamic—as we have seen with Biz and Ro$hi.

Repetition and variation of a narrative element creates meaning. It's a little early for that. In the next chapter, by animating certain scenes in a certain order, we will investigate how series create meaning. For now, let's gain greater exposure to how a series operates, by using your favorite novel and mine, *The Great Gatsby*.

Okay, it may not be your favorite novel, but chances are good that you've read it. And I know that I said we wouldn't use any examples other than the ones we have in common, i.e., Biz and Ro$hi, but series is one area in which multiple examples really can come in handy.

GOING DEEPER: *PDF #3: Fifteen (More) Examples of Series. This PDF contains fifteen more examples of series, drawn from film, modern fantasy, classic literature, and children's books, divided into five types: objects, people, places, phrases and relationships.*

How an Object Becomes a Symbol

When an object repeats and varies, it becomes a symbol. The first occurrence of any series creates foreshadowing. When an object reappears, it is never the same, because its condition and its context have changed—it has varied. There are many object series we could choose from in *The Great Gatsby*, but *The Green Light* series is probably the most celebrated one in the book. Gatsby has been pursuing Daisy for five years until he finally moves into a mansion across the bay from her, thereby potentially becoming her social equal and winning her hand. When Gatsby stretches his arms, he can almost reach the green light at the end of Daisy's dock. He fails to achieve his goal, but he goes to his death still believing in the green light.

I have put *The Green Light* into a series grid, which is the chief action step introduced in this chapter. In the first column is the iteration number, which denotes each time the series occurs. In the second column is the page number, which could be your scene name at this point, given that you only have a messy draft. In the third column is the series name and its type: in this case, an object. The rows in the grid represent the three major times this series repeats and varies, giving you a sense of how those repetitions and variations affect the action.

ITERATION NUMBER	PAGE NUMBER	SERIES NAME: THE GREEN LIGHT SERIES TYPE: OBJECT
1	20–21	...HE STRETCHED OUT HIS ARMS TOWARD THE DARK WATER IN A CURIOUS WAY, AND, FAR AS I WAS FROM HIM, I COULD HAVE SWORN HE WAS TREMBLING. INVOLUNTARILY I GLANCED SEAWARD–AND DISTINGUISHED NOTHING EXCEPT A SINGLE GREEN LIGHT, MINUTE AND FAR AWAY, THAT MIGHT HAVE BEEN THE END OF A DOCK. WHEN I LOOKED ONCE MORE FOR GATSBY HE HAD VANISHED...
2	92	"IF IT WASN'T FOR THE MIST WE COULD SEE YOUR HOME ACROSS THE BAY," SAID GATSBY. "YOU ALWAYS HAVE A GREEN LIGHT THAT BURNS ALL NIGHT AT THE END OF YOUR DOCK." DAISY PUT HER ARM THROUGH HIS ABRUPTLY BUT HE SEEMED ABSORBED IN WHAT HE HAD JUST SAID.
3	180	AND AS I SAT THERE BROODING ON THE OLD, UNKNOWN WORLD, I THOUGHT OF GATSBY'S WONDER WHEN HE FIRST PICKED OUT THE GREEN LIGHT AT THE END OF DAISY'S DOCK. HE HAD COME A LONG WAY TO THIS BLUE LAWN, AND HIS DREAM MUST HAVE SEEMED SO CLOSE THAT HE COULD HARDLY FAIL TO GRASP IT. HE DID NOT KNOW THAT IT WAS ALREADY BEHIND HIM...

How a Person Becomes a Character

The repetitions and variations of series also enable a person to become a character. The first time a person appears in a book establishes his or her identity, and then subsequent developments along a particular narrative arc—a series—reveal his or her character. Many series contribute in some way to our understanding of Gatsby. Since Gatsby is a "round" character, one who evolves throughout the course of the narrative, he has several series that belong to him, including the *Ill-Informed Whispering* series about whether he is a German spy or a bootlegger and the *Gatsby's Education* series that centers on whether he ever was indeed an "Oxford man." The series *Gatsby's Name* reveals very neatly how we process this character over the course of the entire novel. We meet him as Jay Gatsby, but it is eventually revealed that his real name is James Gatz and that he is the son of dirt-poor farmers in North Dakota. As a way of harking back even further, when Gatsby's father shows up for his funeral, he asks, "Where have they got Jimmy?"

How a Place Becomes a Setting

Series also enable a place to become a setting. When multiple scenes take place in the same location, that location gains significance. Place can be used to contrast two locations, such as *West Egg vs. East Egg* in *The Great Gatsby*. These two Long Island communities are, respectively, where Gatsby lives, which is "less fashionable" and full of "crazy fish," and where Tom and Daisy live, which may be more fashionable but "chafed under [its] old euphemisms." Place also can become a part of the plot on its own. The *Gatsby's Swimming Pool* series is a great example of a place series that directly affects the action. The seed that Gatsby hasn't "made use of [the swimming pool] all summer" is first planted halfway through the novel. Toward the very end of the novel, he stops the gardener from draining the pool, because "I've never used that pool all summer." Then, after he is shot dead by Wilson, the garage mechanic, in a case of mistaken revenge, Gatsby ends up floating in the pool.

How a Phrase Becomes a Philosophy

When a phrase is repeated, it can become a message or a mantra. Through the use of series, the repetitions and variations of a phrase can become key to the philosophy of the book. Gatsby's affected expression, "old sport," is one that he first uses to pass himself off as a "man of fine breeding" when actually he is only an "elegant young roughneck." Calling people "old sport," reading "improving book[s]," and practicing "elocution," are all part of Gatsby's lifelong quest to move up the social ladder. Until Tom calls him on it. He sees through Gatsby's pretension, and the *Old Sport* series turns confrontational. Tom asks Gatsby, "All this 'old sport' business. Where'd you pick that up?" Daisy turns around from the mirror, now officially pitched between her two lovers: "Now see here, Tom," she says somewhat desperately, "if you're going to make personal remarks I won't stay here a minute."

How a Relationship Becomes a Dynamic

When a relationship between two or more characters evolves, it has a dynamic effect on the narrative as a whole. At the beginning of *The Great Gatsby*, Fitzgerald wants to link Daisy, the helpless, newly married debutante, with Jay Gatsby, the mysterious millionaire—and he wants to link only those two. We can call the series that bonds them the *Who Has an Innocent Heart (and We Want to See End Up Together)* series. All the telling in the world won't link these eventual lovers in our minds better than does the showing contained in this very subtle series.

Check this out:

[Daisy] laughed again, as if she said something witty, and held my hand for a moment, looking up into my face, promising that there was no one in the world she so much wanted to see. That was a way she had. (p. 9)[5]

[Gatsby] smiled understandingly—much more than understandingly. It was one of those rare smiles with a quality of eternal reassurance in it, that you may come across four or five times in life. It faced— or seemed to face—the whole external world for an instant, and then concentrated on you with an irresistible prejudice in your favor. (p. 48)

• • • • • • • • • • •

5   F. Scott Fitzgerald, *The Great Gatsby* (New York: Scribner, 2004).

Finding Your Series

Finding the series in your work is relatively easy: Just look for the objects, people, places, phrases, and relationships that repeat and vary in your manuscript. What object do you bring back again? Which characters evolve, and how does the reader know that? What places do we revisit, like the scene of the crime when we're closing in on whodunit? What phrases echo through the reader's head, adding a little more meaning to themselves each time they appear? What relationship encounters a rough patch and then straightens things out, becoming stronger than before? You can make a list of those series now. If you get stuck, remember to check out PDF #3: *Fifteen (More) Examples of Series*, to unlock some more possibilities.

If you are writing nonfiction, you can think about the dimensions through which you are choosing to express yourself. Do you use data in a consistent way so that it becomes a part of your presentation? How about case studies? Do those people repeat across chapters, or does just the case study format repeat? What do you call the larger concepts that are spread through your titles and subheads? These are all ways that you build your readers' knowledge rather than just filling their minds with facts.

I'm not trying to get too heavy here. For our practical purposes, the concept of series makes the process of outlining a messy draft more straightforward. Next we will turn to Biz's series and one of the tools that will make writing the method draft easier by offering us steady direction: the series grid.

The Series Grid

When we last left Biz, she had all of her scene packets identified and organized in a provisional order in preparation to begin her second draft. But how did she get there? Yes, well, Ro$hi did it for her... In reality, you might work with an independent editor at this point—especially if you have cut up all your scenes and want a second pair of eyes while you rearrange your scenes into a new order. But that's the thing about fictional examples; there is no Ro$hi. There is only the Ro$hi part of you.

The best way I know of how to put a messy pile of scenes into a dynamic order, informed by analysis, is to create a series grid. If you'd like to experiment with making one of your own, *PDF #4* gives specific instructions. Or, if you just want to understand the general idea for now, we can look at Biz's series grid together.

GOING DEEPER: *PDF #4: Creating a Series Grid From Scratch. This PDF details how to set up the rows of a series grid using scenes and the columns of a series grid using series. It also explains why it's a good idea to start in pencil or, if you're using an electronic spreadsheet, to think of it as being in pencil.*

In the far left column, Biz will put her scene name. But how will she know how far down to place a particular scene? Assuming she isn't going by straight chronological order, she's going to want to determine the sequence and how far apart certain scenes should be spaced.

Some of this is done by intuition about how far into the narrative a scene should go in order to achieve its intended effect. But most of it is done by using the series that are listed in the columns. Let's take the repetitions and variations in the *Drinking* series, for example. If we had read her work-in-progress, we'd see that first Biz drinks, then she doesn't, then she starts drinking again. She knows then that "The Stuff My Mom Would Orchestrate an Honor Killing For" scene likely goes in the first third of the narrative (drinking) or the last third of the narrative (return to drinking).

SCENE NAME	DRINKING	PLACES I'VE LIVED	BOYFRIENDS
THE ABSOLUTE WORST HUMAN TO LIVE WITH & ROOMMATE ETIQUETTE 101		✓	
THE STUFF MY MOM WOULD ORCHESTRATE AN HONOR KILLING FOR	✓		
MY OFFICE WAS THE OFFICE BEFORE THE OFFICE WAS THE OFFICE			
WHEN DO WE START YELLING IN THE STREET			✓
THIS APARTMENT WAS SUPPOSED TO FIX MY LIFE		✓	
A GENTLE DISCUSSION ABOUT MY CRAZY ULTIMATUMS			✓
THE SCORPIONS WILL EAT YOUR FEET			
LIVING SOMEWHERE FOR MORE THAN A YEAR FOR THE FIRST TIME IN A DECADE		✓	

Since Biz is aiming to write an uplifting tale, she's going to assign that scene to the first third, because by the time she's returned to drinking she's wiser about it. As I mentioned, Biz doesn't want to tell the events of her story in the exact order that they happened; rather, she wants to rearrange the events in order to enhance the meaning of the ones she selects.

GOING DEEPER: *PDF #5: Chronological vs. Narrative Order. These are the two orders in which events can be presented to the reader. In narrative order, events are not presented chronologically (the order in which they happened), but rather are rearranged for dramatic or psychological effect. Consult this PDF for examples of both types of order.*

Biz can apply the same logic we used in the *Drinking* series, to the *Places I Have Lived In* series. Remember that she forgot the "Roommate Etiquette 101" scene but remembered "The Absolute Worst Human to Live With" scene? (You can hear how these have the same exact, edgy tone, can't you?) The uberscene that will combine these two scenes will be presented before the "This Apartment Was Supposed to Fix My Life" scene. In order to gain clarity, she moves out of wherever she was, but she only gets partway, and she can keep track of this on her grid. Eventually there will be a scene titled "Living Somewhere for More than a Year for the First Time in a Decade."

The series grid includes both those scenes in which a series first occurs as foreshadowing and the scenes where it repeats and varies. Take the series, Biz's *Boyfriends.* The scene "When Do We Start Yelling in the Street?" comes partway into the narrative, because by that time Biz has already been burned by a previous bad relationship. That scene goes before "A Gentle Discussion About My Crazy Ultimatums," again, as Biz evolves toward wisdom.

In this way, Biz is putting the scenes from her memoir in a new order by using her series to help her discover connections. If she comes across a scene that doesn't belong to any series, such as "Looking at My Credit Card Balances Is My After-Work Hobby," she needs to hold it off the grid for the time being.

I can hear Biz complaining: "*Drinking*? *The Places I Have Lived*? *Boyfriends*? This sounds like the pathetic memoir of any thirty-one-year-old. What about a series like *My Tortured Catholic Upbringing* or *Finding Myself Through Yoga*? When do things get good?"

Biz's series can demonstrate as much creativity as she wants, but as you may have noticed in *PDF #3*, a tangible series is almost always better than an abstract series, both for your sake as the crafter of the work and for the sake of the readers that are trying their best to follow along with you.

It gets "good" when series begin to interact, and eventually collide. In Biz's case, the *Drinking* series and the *Boyfriends* series intersect frequently: Some boyfriends don't drink, but one boyfriend gets her back into drinking and it isn't the end of the world. She looks forward to a time when she'll no longer drink; will her drinking boyfriend still be in the picture then? That's part of the drama that keeps you reading…

When you put your scene list into a series grid, these are the kinds of connections that emerge. Will it be perfect? Sometimes your placement of a scene in the method draft will be slightly out of sync; those series developments that don't fit quite perfectly can be told as flashbacks or memories, they can be cut or changed, or they can be introduced by a voice that says, "Relapse is part of the cure…"

Remember what Rilke said: "Live the questions now." The nature of your questions has likely changed during the process to this point. Some questions, such as "What does the main female character do for a living?" and "What would she have done to arouse the suspicions she is under?" may have been answered just by what you have learned over time through pantsing. And some questions will remain.

And that's okay. The series grid is just an outline, and you can change it at any time. It has certain advantages over other types of outlines with which you may be familiar. For one thing, it is an outline based on what you have done, not those complex outlines before you've ever written a word.

The other main thing I like about the series grid is that it is spatial in nature. It looks nothing like those outlines we were taught in school, you know, the legal form:

I.
  A.
      1.
      2.
  B.
      1.
II.

I don't know about you, but I don't find that kind of linear list very inspiring. I would rather see everything that I am dealing with spread out in front of me in a non-hierarchical fashion. Using a series grid for your second draft, on the other hand, invites you to think about weaving series together, about how much should be going on in one scene in order to hit the right emotional tone. It helps you to ensure consistency with your various narrative arcs, become aware of any gaping holes, and create complex emotional, psychological, and philosophical effects.

But don't just take my word for it.

J.K. Rowling's Series Grid

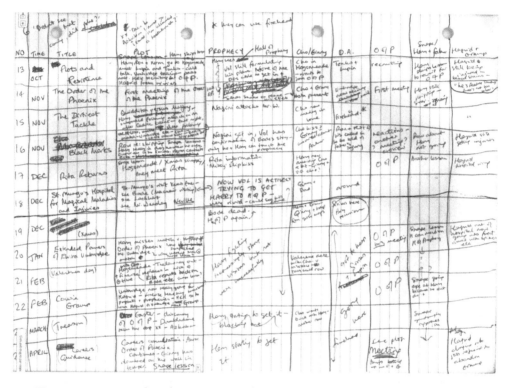

This is J.K. Rowling's series grid from book five of the Harry Potter series, *Harry Potter and the Order of the Phoenix*. I unpack this grid at great length in chapter five of *BA*, a chapter I co-authored with C.S. Plocher; you can also dig into the details on C.S.'s four-part blog series here.[6]

In brief, Rowling's first column contains her chapter number (we have been using Biz's scene name in the same way to mark progress through the narrative). After that, she has a time stamp to help her

6 http://writelikerowling.com/2013/10/08/rowling-outline-part-one/

keep track of when the action takes place, from October through April of one school year. After that, she has seven columns that correspond to the various series that she wants to weave together in the given time and place of a particular scene.

Joseph Heller's Series Grid

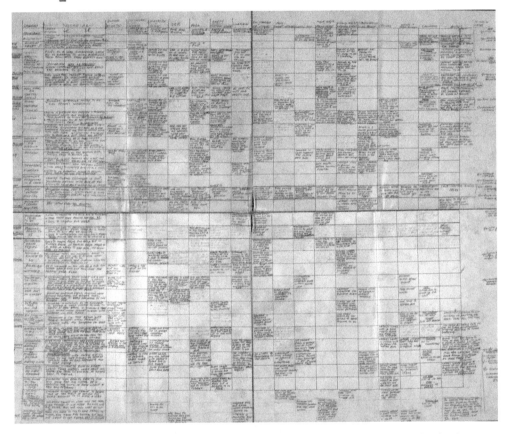

Image used courtesy of Robert D. Farber University Archives & Special Collections Department, Brandeis University

These grids get increasingly crazier. This is Joseph Heller's series grid for his novel *Catch-22*. I saw this in person at the Brandeis University Library, and one thing I noticed is that it is all written in pencil. There are smudge marks, partial erasures, and things being moved around... meaning this outline is like a map, as we were saying earlier. Heller updated it as he got closer and closer to shore. It is a tool, and its value lies in being used. Even after you begin the method draft (soon!), you can keep track of all the information that comes to you by keeping the grid updated: "grid maintenance," we like to call it.

If you would like a detailed description of Heller's series grid, you can go to chapter six of *BA*. But you can also look at it from here (and don't worry, your grid does not need to be this complex). If you look at an individual column, you can see that any given series doesn't occur in every chapter. That would be overload. The first time a series appears is what we have referred to as foreshadowing. Then the series disappears for a little while so that we can long for it. This is where suspense comes in: When a series is gone from our conscious mind but not our subconscious mind and we expect it to come back. When a series is gone from even our subconscious mind before it reappears, that is how the author creates surprise or even administers shock.

When you see white space on your series grid, you have to ask, "Am I building suspense for this element, or have I actually forgotten to put in an important piece?" If the latter, you can add it to your list of missing scenes and write those scenes any time you feel inspired. And even if you don't feel totally inspired, it's good to give a missing scene at least one messy-draft whack before you get too far into the method draft.

Whether you create a full-fledged series grid or not, you have likely become aware of some of your series while reading this chapter. I can promise you that series awareness pays off in the long run, especially as you make your way toward the last major task of preparing for the method draft: finding your theme.

CHAPTER FIVE

The Method Draft, Part III: Finding Your Theme

Scene, series, and theme. Biz has examined her scenes and identified each of them as good, bad, forgotten, or missing. She has listed her series and used those series to reorder her scenes and enhance their connections. Now the last thing Biz needs is to find her theme, to suffuse every scene with the one thing that her book is about, because her book can only be about one thing.

*IN FACT, I HAVE PUT THAT IN ALL THREE OF MY BOOKS. WHAT WOULD POSSESS SOMEONE TO DO THAT?

I say that a lot. Often enough that one of my students told me, "Your book can only be about one thing...I think that's *your* one thing." You know students. Another one asked me, "What about two things? Can my book be about two things?" To which I replied, "Yes. Provided those two things are about one thing."

How do you go about finding your theme, and what value does it bring to writing the method draft? Let's take those questions one at a time.

Four Ways of Finding Your Theme

In this chapter we will introduce four ways of finding your theme, each a little more complex than the next. As a first way of finding your theme, you can use what you thought you were writing about all along. Just write one sentence that describes your work as you understood it when you were starting out. I am not in the camp that says the writer has no idea what she or he is really doing, that it all exists in the subconscious, and that the reader or a critic is actually in a better position to say what a book is about.

I won't go that far. But I will say that the book should be somewhat different by the end of the messy draft than it was before you started writing; otherwise, you haven't taken full advantage of pantsing.

Concepts change as we complete them. I liken it to the movement of the hands of a clock (on the kind of clock that has hands). What you set out to do is your theme at 12 o'clock. By writing the messy draft, you move the hour hand forward to 1 o'clock. Now we can look at your theme at 1 o'clock and, during the method draft, consciously push it forward to 2 o'clock.

The second way of finding your theme is to consider what you actually think about the first theme you wrote down. Is this theme something you can get behind now? One method-draft mantra might be:

Believe it... Or, change it.

It's sort of the adult version of "Are we still having fun?" Is this work reflective (and therefore worthy) of what I want to bring to the world?

The third way of finding your theme is a little bit more complex. It involves ranking your series by order of importance and then describing each of the top four series in its own sentence. Ideally, these four sentences will describe what changes in each series. You then reduce those four sentences to two sentences and finally to a one-sentence statement of what your book is about (because your book can only be about one thing).

> **GOING DEEPER:** *PDF #6: Finding Your Theme. This PDF follows one of my students, Kimberly, as she finds her theme by twice reducing the number of sentences that describe her novel. When she is able to circle that one key phrase that represents her theme it will help determine the direction of her revision from messy draft to method draft.*

The fourth way of finding your theme is to find it sitting right in the middle of your book; the reason this is more complex is that you may not be able to find the theme in this way until after you've tried using the first three ways. You can use a combination of all four ways, or you can pick a couple of them and go forward with those. Remember, the point of any action step is not to make work for you. It's to see if they help—and, if they do, to use them reliably.

Theme of *The Great Gatsby*

In the case of *The Great Gatsby*, I engaged the first two ways of finding a theme by reading some of Fitzgerald's descriptions of his intentions while he wrote the earlier drafts of the novel that he called *Trimalchio* at the time (or *Trimalchio in West Egg*). I used the third way to identify the four series that I deemed most relevant to understanding the character of Gatsby (*Old Sport*, *Gatsby's Name*, *Ill-Informed Whispering*, and *Gatsby's Education*) and wrote a sentence for each of them. Then I combined those four sentences into two sentences and then one sentence. When I was done, I found something very similar to the result (but better) on page 88 of *The Great Gatsby* itself:

> *"Americans, while occasionally willing to be serfs, have*
> *always been obstinate about being peasantry."*

GOING DEEPER: *PDF #7: Seven Themes from Well-Known Narratives. Consult this PDF to review the themes of the novels* Harry Potter and the Order of the Phoenix, Catch-22, *and* Anna Karenina, *the films* Slumdog Millionaire *and* The Social Network, *and the children's stories* Corduroy *and* The Ugly Duckling.

Client and Student Examples of Theme

Let's look at a few examples of the one thing a book can be about from some of my clients and students over the years. In the first two cases, the authors worked through a variety of exercises and then found their themes located right in the material.

> *"I found myself, and my man found me."*

This is kind of the standard theme of all chick lit, right? Yet it wasn't until she knew what she was looking for that my client found this already in her book. Here is another theme from the middle of a memoir:

"It's not how you fall in life, it's how you pick yourself up."

Now you may think that's a cliché. It may be a cliché. But the value of a good theme does not come from it being original. It comes from it being true to your experience. Like, do you believe that? ("It's not how you fall in life...") I do; I think that's true. Which is important if I'm not only going to write a whole book about it, but especially if I'm going to have to write three drafts of that book.

The originality comes from the clothing we put on it. Like:

> *"How a girl goes from being a drunk, crying*
> *lesbian to just being a drunk lesbian."*

You can see the change in that, right? She might be all set now. Thanks to Jenn and Brown University for this example; Jenn just blurted this out in class one day when trying to describe how her work had evolved from her initial conception (the second way of finding your theme).

Let's look at one more theme. Like the first two authors, Rich found his theme right in the middle (on page 192) of his manuscript in progress:

> *"To the outside world, the Navy may appear to be*
> *black and white; to the officers and men that served,*
> *the Navy was a thousand shades of grey."*

That is pretty long (twenty-eight words) as themes go, but it is still a one-sentence statement of what the author's book is about. Technically, your theme can be as short as two words, because that is how short a sentence can be (subject plus object).

Using the Target

When you have your theme, we are ready to answer the second question that was posed at the beginning of this chapter: "What value does knowing your theme bring to the method draft?" However you found your theme, we can now use logic to align the construction of your work in a way that expresses what you actually want to say. Remember, the method draft is all about making sense.

One of my favorite ways of doing this is to put the theme in the bull's-eye of an archery target and arrange the series and scenes around it, closer to or farther from the theme, based on their perceived relevance.

This is Rich's target from class (that's why it looks a little bit like the Rosetta Stone). Scribbled on it are series such as *Homosexuality*. You can see how that would be a shade of grey in the Navy, right? "Don't ask; don't tell." That's got shade of grey written all over it.

The scene named "Soviets" is another great example of a shade of grey. In this scene, one submarine rescues another submarine from freezing cold waters...but it is a Russian sub that rescues a U.S. sub at the height of the Cold War, showing that the allegiance these submariners felt for each other was stronger than contrived political differences.

Not everything needs to change.

That's a good method-draft mantra. For many scenes and series, all you need to do is make them better. That's one of my favorite things to write in the margin when I am editing a client's work, "Make this better." You may have started pantsing your first draft with very close to nothing, but now you have something. Remember, you are taking the best parts up a level—not ten.

OR JUST, "MAKE BETTER."

Using the archery target is a great way to prepare for the method draft, because it helps you to assess the importance of some of the elements of your manuscript in relationship to each other, like adjusting the mix in music so that certain instruments become more prominent and others fade enough so that they are no longer overwhelming. What should you do if a scene or a series doesn't land on the target at all? Well, you should get rid of it, of course.

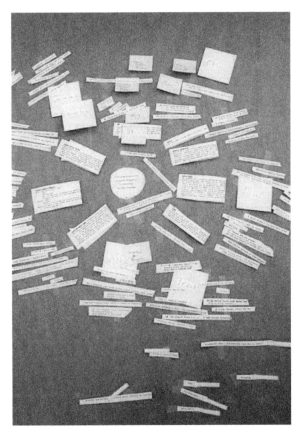

Jeanette has taken the extra step of tagging the narrative elements that don't fit her theme with these heavy green sticky notes so that they can never again convince her that they should be included. What's already written can be very convincing, but this is what William Faulkner meant when he said, "Kill all your darlings." Now is as good a time as any. Some of those bad and forgotten scenes that we discovered in chapter three of this book are going to have to be left behind. Revision is about limitation. And besides, you have to make room for the missing scenes you have yet to write and the series you are going to trace majestically as you nail your theme.

[Watch Video Seven: Biz Hits the Target]

BIZ: I GOT IT! I GOT MY THEME!

BIZ: DON'T YOU WANNA KNOW WHAT IT IS?

BIZ: OH I GET IT, THIS IS LIKE A ZEN THING. I KEEP IT TO MYSELF AND IT GROWS IN POWER.
SO NOW WHAT? IF THE FIRST DRAFT IS THE EASY PART, THE SECOND DRAFT IS WHAT?
THE HARD PART?

RO$HI: ACTUALLY THE HARD PART IS QUERYING AGENTS. BUT SERIOUSLY FOLKS, NOW THAT YOU HAVE YOUR THEME, YOU CAN DISCARD THOSE SERIES THAT DON'T MAKE THE TARGET.

RO$HI: YOU CAN DECIDE WHICH OF YOUR BAD AND FORGOTTEN SCENES YOU WILL REWRITE AND WHICH YOU WILL JUST LEAVE BEHIND. AND YOU CAN FILL OUT YOUR SERIES GRID TO KEEP TRACK OF EVERYTHING AND MAKE SENSE OF THE BIGGER PICTURE.

BIZ: WELL, HOW DO I KNOW IF I HAVE THE RIGHT NUMBER OF SERIES? WOULDN'T IT BE EASIER TO JUST FOLLOW A FORMULA? CAN'T YOU COME DOWN THE MOUNTAIN WITH ME?

RO$HI: LET'S NOT GET AHEAD OF OURSELVES. AT THE END OF THE SECOND DRAFT WE'RE NOT YET READY TO RELEASE THIS TO THE WORLD. NEXT, WE NEED TO FIND YOU SOME BETA READERS.

Write That Method Draft!

You might not have completed all of the exercises I have recommended in preparing for the method draft. Or you might have completed even more exercises, including drawing arcs of your series and laying them on top of each other to get a sense of the overall narrative arc (*see PDF #8*).

> GOING DEEPER: *PDF #8: The Series Arc. In BA, I introduced three tools; in this book, we have talked about the grid and the target. For more information about the third tool, graphing multiple narrative arcs to foster connections and establish pace, consult this PDF.*

What matters now is that we harness the right method-draft attitudes, beginning with taking the word *rewriting* out of our vocabulary. That is not what we are doing; we are revising, re-visioning our work as we complete our second drafts.

In fact, I don't recommend rewriting at all. Wherever possible, if I have really gotten something right in my messy draft—a good scene—I will copy and paste as much of it as possible into my method draft. How refreshing! That's done.

Because, as we saw earlier, we have work to do. We have bad and forgotten scenes to examine closely and make decisions about. We have exciting possibilities, either newly imagined or just remembered, to explore. Once we see the nature of the work we have to do ahead of us, the only thing that can stop us is ourselves.

Sometimes during the second draft, writers will encounter something that I call "The Tyranny of the First Draft." This passing rain cloud basically privileges everything that you've done before over what you're going to do in the future. I think it stems from the fact that creative stuff just arrives; so because you don't know where it comes from, you wonder if it will come again. Last month or last year it wasn't here but now that it's sitting in the printer, it becomes better than anything else you could ever do.

In one of the deleted scenes, Ro$hi tells Biz, "But we don't have anything to fear, because your creativity is inexhaustible. Do you believe that?" To which Biz responds, "Yes! I guess..."

That's good enough. Just as you got permission to write a draft that was messy, and just as you got permission to stop writing, I now give you permission to write the method draft while knowing that you are going to get some of it wrong. You are also going to get some of it startlingly right.

Here are a few more mantras to keep you company while you write your method draft:

* *what else would you like me to tell you?*
* *take your opportunities*
* *weave it in*
* *you don't have to reinvent the wheel*
* *let the connections emerge*
* *go further*
* *break through*
* *link cause and effect*

* *it doesn't have to be perfect yet*
* *add in good new stuff*
* *remember your mission*
* *sometimes leaving the great stuff alone is a win*
* *where it needs it, you will get it*
* *go on, if it's done*
* *pull it off*

"I never do any correcting or revising while in the process of writing. Let's say I write a thing out any old way, and then, after it's cooled off—I let it rest for a while…I see it with a fresh eye. Then I have a wonderful time of it. I just go to work on it with the ax…. When I'm revising, I use a pen and ink to make changes, cross out, insert. The manuscript looks wonderful afterwards…. Then I retype, and in the process of retyping I make more changes."

— *HENRY MILLER*

CHAPTER SIX

The Polished Draft, Part I: Role of the Beta Reader

Writing can get lonely. The further you go out on your personal edge during the method draft, the lonelier it gets. Plus, writing is an act of communication. It isn't really completed until you have a reader (or ten thousand). For these reasons, plus wanting to prove someone wrong, plus being so happy about something you've created that you just have to share it with other people, plus making sure you're not crazy, plus multiple other reasons, it is only natural that you would want to show your work to other people.

The question is when. You may have worked with an independent editor around the time you were cutting up your scenes. Or your work may have remained between you and you. Just because writing entails a certain amount of loneliness, it doesn't mean that loneliness has to turn into a lack of confidence that breaks our concentration. If you wait to seek out other readers until the method draft is complete, you will have strengthened the work so that it can take a little pushback. By that time, you already know some of what you tried that didn't work, so you aren't quite as impressionable as you were after the messy draft. You can remain at your maximum openness while soliciting the honest feedback of your first readers in a structured process.

Now that you are preparing to create the third and final draft of your work, the polished draft, it is time to find these other people you can trust and ask them for their input—regardless of whether you go in the directions they suggest. I know this isn't how a lot of writers' groups work. Often you have to finish the first part of a first draft and then read it to the whole class. All I'm saying is, I've seen a lot of bad come out of that. Eventually, yes—eventually your work can leave the inner circle and travel outward through less familiar hands...and into the hands of total strangers. Eek!

In between the multitudes and lonely old you, there lies room for a very special breed of individual that we in the business call the "beta reader." I don't know where that name comes from. I get that it comes from the first user of a product, the beta tester. That still doesn't explain why, if your first readers are your beta readers, who is the alpha reader? You?

For our purposes, we'll define a beta reader this way:

A beta reader is an individual who reads your work before it is finished and offers you feedback.

Not just any feedback—constructive, motivating, eye-opening feedback to help you prepare for your third and final draft, the polished draft. Well, that's the way it's supposed to work, anyway. For most of this chapter, we will talk about how many beta readers you should have, where you can find them, and what kind of questions you should ask them in order to get the most out of the process. But before we get to those details, let's pause for a moment to consider what kind of a person we can trust to fulfill the role of beta reader.

Objectivity Is a Myth

*PEOPLE OVERUSE THE SAYING "IT'S A PRIVILEGE, IT'S AN HONOR," BUT SOME THINGS ARE.

When we ask someone to beta read for us, it is an honor. It is also a lot of work, but we will pay them back, as we will see a little later on in this book. We often think that when we are looking for beta readers we are seeking someone who is objective, but objectivity is a myth. No one can read a work without having reactions to it, and those reactions are based on the reader's personal history, taste, and aspirations.

The question is: How conscious of all that can a beta reader be? Here we might borrow strategies from therapy: Can your beta reader make "I" statements? You know like:

> "When I read _____(x)_____, it made me think of
> _____(y)_____, and that is why I think it might
> be too _____(z)_____. You don't have to agree
> with me, but that's where I'm coming from..."

Now, that's a worthwhile beta reader, someone who doesn't pretend to offer objective feedback but rather transparently subjective feedback.

This returns us to the neutral audience we discussed earlier, which was symbolized by Ro$hi's blank "book face." Neutrality has no agenda.

Our beta readers don't have to worry about the "praise sandwich"—you know, positive responses followed by possibly controversial suggestions followed by more praise. They don't have to puff themselves up because we've told them we want them to be "brutally honest" with us. On the other hand, we aren't looking for necessarily kind readers either. All of that is too much work.

Or rather, it is the wrong kind of work. Those approaches are too similar to the cheerleader and the critic that we discussed in chapter one of this book: the cheerleader who says, "I've never read anything like your book," and the critic who says, "You're working in a pretty crowded field..." Those are two sides of the same tortured psychic coin that can lead to nightmares.

[Watch Video Eight: Nightmare Train]

(Author's note: This one you really have to watch. I've watched it ten times and I'm still not sure I get it.)

BIZ: WHAT THE HECK IS GOING ON? WHY DOESN'T ANYONE WANT TO SIT NEXT TO ME?

I GOT A MONSTER HEADACHE.

RO$HI? IS THAT YOU?

THALIA: THERE'S AN AWFUL LOT OF MEN ON THIS TRAIN,
DON'T YOU THINK?

 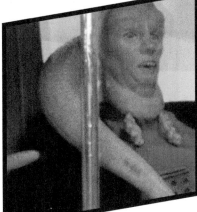 

MELPOMENE:
WELL, YOU'VE READ HER BOOK.
DOESN'T IT MAKE SENSE? WHAT DO YOU EXPECT
FROM SOMEONE WHO PRACTICALLY LIVES OFF SHOCK VALUE?

BIZ: WHO ARE YOU GUYS? YOU'VE READ MY BOOK? WHY DO I LOOK LIKE THIS?

THALIA: YOU'RE A WRITER NOW, HONEY. IT'S NATURAL TO
FEEL A LITTLE ALIENATED. BUT DON'T WORRY ABOUT THAT.
LOOK AT THE BIG PICTURE. YOU WROTE A BOOK! NOT
EVERYBODY WRITES A BOOK.

MELPOMENE: THESE DAYS THEY DO. DO YOU HAVE
ANY IDEA HOW MANY PEOPLE SELF-PUBLISHED A BOOK LAST YEAR?

THALIA: STOP, YOU'RE SCARING HER. WE'RE NOT EVEN AT THAT POINT IN THE PROCESS YET.

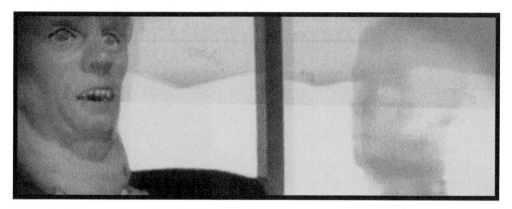

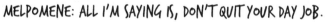

MELPOMENE: ALL I'M SAYING IS, DON'T QUIT YOUR DAY JOB.

THALIA: I THINK YOU'RE A BRAVE SOUL. YOUR WORK MAKES ME WANT TO WEEP... IN A GOOD WAY.

MELPOMENE: OH, BOY... AGAIN WITH THE WEEPING. COME ON, THIS IS OUR STOP.

BIZ: IS IT MY STOP, TOO?

THALIA: NOT YET. YOU JUST KEEP UP THE GOOD WORK, HONEY! YOU'LL KNOW WHEN IT'S TIME.

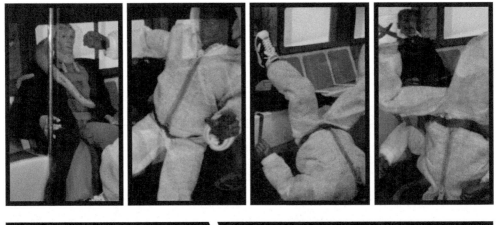

BIZ: RO$HI? IS THAT YOU?

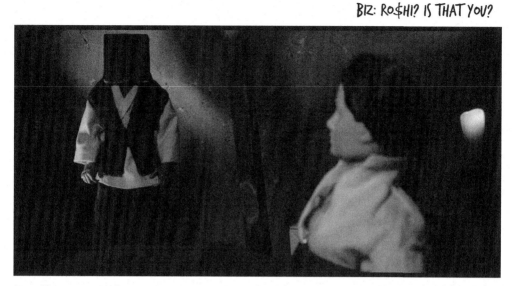

BIZ: THERE WERE TWO ANDROIDS...A HUSBAND AND A WIFE, I THINK. THEY LOOKED EXACTLY ALIKE BUT HAD DIFFERENT IDEAS.

BIZ: ONE OF THEM THOUGHT EVERYTHING I DID WAS GREAT. I LIKED HER MORE... WERE THOSE MY BETA READERS?

RO$HI: NO, NO. THAT WAS THE CRITIC AND THE CHEERLEADER. THEY'RE HARD TO AVOID. YOUR BETA READERS ARE SOMETHING COMPLETELY DIFFERENT. AND UNLIKE THOSE TWO, BETA READERS CAN ACTUALLY BE HELPFUL.

How Many Beta Readers Should I Have?

This is another one of those questions (like how many drafts of a work you should do) that you would think doesn't have an answer. The answer does vary based on the length of your work, your timetable, and the genre, but I propose that your number of beta readers be between three and seven.

If you have less than three, you may tend to weight the individual feedback too strongly. This is especially true if you start with only one beta reader. Sometimes one or two are all we can find, or all we feel like we can trust for the time being, or because we aren't quite ready yet to call ourselves writers, even though we have a full method draft to share.

On the other end of the spectrum, I don't think you need more than seven beta readers. Remember, these are not your reader readers, where, yeah, you want hundreds of them. As we will see, we aren't looking for consensus anyway—this is not a democracy, so it isn't like the more people we get to vote shows that our system is working. If you have more than seven beta readers, you may feel that the air traffic control is getting out of hand.

Where Do I Find My Beta Readers?

WELL, YOU COULD HIRE AN INDEPENDENT EDITOR, which is what I do for a living. Okay, that's my only plug, I think, so far. Maybe the second. Anyway, there are other options: Many writers join critique groups, which they find through online forums, writing workshops, or literary organizations. The best thing about finding beta readers this way is that there is usually some automatic exchange at play—my manuscript for your manuscript—which, as we will see below, is very important.

Critique groups have grown up a lot over the past several years I have noticed as I travel across the country. Maybe I'm just used to college, where everybody is either trying to get laid or trying to express their latent frustrations—not a lot of transparently subjective feedback going to come from either of those situations, it doesn't sound like.

As I said in the "Find a Neutral Audience" tip back in chapter one, you can even involve your friends and family, provided that you read them the riot act first: you can't say, "I love it" and you can't say, "I guess I'm just not your audience," i.e., "I hate it." You have to follow the instructions we are going to give you just like everyone else.

One final thought: It is a good idea to select beta readers from a pool of likely readers in your genre. I recently heard the story of a writer who asked a friend of hers to beta read her novel. As it turns out, the friend was an avid reader of nonfiction, so she wanted her questions about the story to be answered on the same page in which they came up. Which is, um, not the way stories work, so that wasn't going to do.

There Has to Be an Equal Energy Exchange

One of my friends wrote her entire master's thesis on the philosophy of giving and receiving. I'll break it down for you here: There has to be both. Make sure you are giving something of value in return to your beta readers because you are going to ask something of substance from them. Maybe you are beta reading their books, or you are offering free PR or SEO expertise, or you are dog sitting for them next week, or you are paying them. You can't afford to be unappreciative of your beta readers, so ask them how you can best return the favor.

The Beta Reader Questionnaire

Here we come to the basics of what you are asking your beta readers to do. Throughout the three-draft process, you have had questions. Some of those questions have since resolved themselves; some of them didn't turn out to be questions at all. And some of those questions you still have.

As you prepare to write your polished draft, the beta reader questionnaire is a vehicle for you to ask those remaining questions. How to phrase these questions to receive the greatest benefit from your beta readers is where we are heading next. Sometimes even the way in which you ask the question gives you a clue to the answer you are seeking. But first, my advice: When you ask a question, listen to the answer.

It's hard, I know. You've sent off your work, and now it's out there. Will you be rejected? And if someone doesn't get it, will you decide they are not as smart as you thought they were, whereas if they love what you've done, well then you're bound to be besties now...? I have wasted good time popping in and out of these rabbit holes, when all I really needed to do was listen to someone tell me something about my writing that I didn't already know. If we've taken the method draft as far as we can on our own, all that's left is to prepare ourselves to be surprised by the feedback we receive. That puts us in the sweet spot of the beta-reading experience.

Format of the Questionnaire

* Ask your beta readers **ten specific questions**.
* Suggest they write **a paragraph or two in response** to each question—less, if they think they can cover it in a couple of lines, or more, if they get inspired.

* Set *a reasonable date* for reading your manuscript and returning the questionnaire, based on the length of your work and the amount of time you've been on their calendar.
* Remind readers that your work **has not been copy edited yet** and therefore they should not worry about grammar or punctuation. (Why copy edit a paragraph when the entire thing might be coming out anyway? Copy editing comes later.)

Types of Questions to Ask Beta Readers

Most questions on a beta reader questionnaire fall into one of three categories: content, pacing, and marketing.

Content

For content questions, you can ask my favorite:

> *"What scenes do you remember the best?"*

Or any of these variations:

> *"Did any character strike you as particularly memorable?"*
> *"Were any of the characters too 'over the top'? (i.e., memorable in a bad way)?"*
> *"Did you particularly identify with any one character's opinions? Which one, and how?"*

Most content questions, thus, are really "more or less" questions:

> *"Less violence?"*
> *"More sex?"*
> *"Did you have any questions that weren't answered adequately by the current manuscript?"*

Pacing

The second major category of beta reader questions addresses the issues of pace and structure. These questions are a great way to get ideas about your manuscript, as well as ideas for your manuscript.

> *"Did any sections of the manuscript feel underdeveloped?"*
> *"Which parts did you want to skip?"*
> *"Where did you feel there was an emotional payoff?"*
> *"Did the answers to your questions come later than you were looking for them?"*

Marketing

The last major category of beta reader questions is marketing. If you are writing nonfiction, you will have to craft a book proposal to go along with your manuscript. If you are writing fiction, you will need good supporting material for your query letter and synopsis. Even if you are planning to self-publish, you will still need ad copy for the back cover of the book, your author web presence, and other marketing materials.

> **GOING DEEPER:** *PDF #9: Brainstorming Your Book's Support Materials. This PDF contains brainstorming questions that will help you to generate the standard front matter for a nonfiction book proposal, including Overview/About the Audience, About the Author, Marketing & Promotion, and Competitive Titles, as well as your query letter to literary agents and smaller publishers.*

Marketing questions that may help you to craft these documents include the following:

"If you were to describe this book to someone in one paragraph, how would you do it?"
(helps with Overview/About the Audience)
"Who would you recommend this book to and why?"
(helps with About the Audience)
"What authors' works did it remind you of?"
(helps with Competitive Titles)

To conclude the questionnaire, you might include one catch-all question, such as:

"What question did I forget to ask?

This gambit, or its variation, "Anything else you'd like to mention?" can put your beta readers on the spot and be difficult to answer. At the same time, they will likely appreciate the sentiment: *I'm giving you some questions to help you focus your reactions, but I am of course open to whatever crosses your mind.*

For my first book, I had a beta reader who totally blew off the questionnaire and instead wrote me a three-page letter that contained an idea so different from anything I had considered that I had to write an entirely new chapter just to address it.

*I FORGIVE YOU, LIZA.

One final note on the types of questions you can ask on your questionnaire: If you are getting a specialized read, you will want to ask more specific questions. For example, you may be having your book read to make sure that it adheres to the compliance rules of your particular industry. You may be having your book read by a cop or a lawyer, for procedural accuracy. You may be having it read by a member of the culture about which you are writing, if you do not belong to that culture. All of these questionnaires will need to be more tailored than one for a more general beta read.

Pat's Beta Reader Questionnaire

Below, you can see a questionnaire that I put together with a client. Pat is a neuroscientist who has become aware, through her work, that midlife for human beings has greatly expanded. For our ancestors, it was a

Pat's Beta Reader Questionnaire

1. Did you enjoy having these tales divided into sections: self, couples, etc. or would you have preferred to simply read the tales as an entire collection?

2. If you liked the division into sections, did the order of those sections (self>couples>families>community) work for you?

3. Did you enjoy the introductions, or would you have preferred only one introduction followed by all of the tales, or would you have liked to just read the tales with no introductions at all?

4. Did you want more or less science in the introductions?

5. What midlife situations or dilemmas, if any, did you feel were missing?

6. What midlife situations or dilemmas did you want more of?

7. Which three tales were your least favorite, and why?

8. Which three tales spoke to you the most clearly, and why?

9. If you were going to recommend this book to someone what would you say to them?

10. Did the title and subtitle suit the book in your eyes?

Again, thank you very much for your efforts to assist me.
Above all, I am very grateful for your time.

mere flash of time between the end of youth and the onset of old age. Now midlife can span from age forty to beyond age seventy. And here was Pat's unique realization: Our cultures have left us virtually no fairy tales that address that phase of life. So Pat set out to write some.

By the end of her method draft, Pat had thirty-two tales in hand, so part of the content section of her questionnaire was designed to help her to whittle down the number of tales:

"Which three tales were your least favorite and why?"
"Which three tales spoke to you the most clearly and why?"

Because Pat was a neuroscientist, she had divided the tales into four groups and introduced each group with a different essay about the science of aging: How dementia sets in and, conversely, how one can increase neuroplasticity (the ability to form new cerebral connections throughout life).

Question #4 was, thus, perhaps the most controversial pacing question:

"Did you want more or less science in the introductions?"

One reader was emphatic: "More science! And footnotes, and suggestions for further reading!"

Another reader was just as emphatic: "Boooo! No science! I almost put the whole book down because of the science!"

Now you might think that Pat didn't learn anything from these responses, with a hung jury of sorts. But again, this isn't a democracy, and we aren't looking for consensus. We are looking for resonance. We are looking for what sticks with us, in that yucky-but-still-somehow-uplifting fashion that convinces you there is a change to be made. Pat knew in her heart of hearts that the science had to come out; they were one of her darlings that would have to be killed.

It all boils down to resonance. I mean, you asked. You placed yourself on the road to finding out what you think. It can become confusing because, while your beta readers are accompanying you on the trip, you are still driving. Recently, I found my notes from the beta read of my first book. I had scrawled in the margin, "Everybody wants me to sound like more of an authority, unless it's in places where they don't agree with me, then they want me to be more open-ended."

The beta reader experience is scary, because you put yourself out there and your method draft is not perfect. That's the point; you still have the polished draft to go. The messy draft is about getting it down, and the method draft is about making sense. But the polished draft is about making it good.

What we need to do right now is take it all in: the off-base remarks and the right-on-target remarks—we just listen. We try to stay neutral, or at least be transparently subjective, just as we are asking our beta readers to be.

When a writer and a beta reader work together most productively, it is as if the pair gets away altogether from the notion of *constructive feedback* and instead engages in what may be called *reconstructive feedback*. Those beta reader responses can contribute powerful information to a writer's process, and help prepare for the creation of that third and final draft, which we call the polished draft.

CHAPTER SEVEN

The Polished Draft, Part II: Putting Together a Punch List

B y way of recap, the first draft, or messy draft, is all about getting it down. The second draft, or method draft, is about making sense. We are now about to begin the third draft, the polished draft. This draft is all about making it good.

In the previous chapter, I mentioned the beta readers that I gathered together for my first book. We actually started as a focus group, and then everybody split off to complete their individual assignments. Except Liza. When I gathered the feedback from my other beta readers, I compiled the responses that resonated and started putting together a punch list for my final draft.

I tried to make this list as comprehensive as possible. No sense mailing it in. If an idea was legitimately a good one, I had every intention of weaving it in. If an idea was legitimately a bad one, I tried to remember that polished-draft mantra:

Make decisions

I have an editor friend who once described the book she was working on by saying, "It only has to be so good." I prefer to stop at nothing on the punch list, to make something feel so full it is irresistible.

I also used the folder of notes that I had been keeping the whole time. This was my

treasure trove for later ornamentation: notes I had taken on my phone, which I later printed out, notes I had taken while writing about things I just couldn't get to yet, ideas I had covered in two iterations but that needed that magical third iteration, and so forth. In fact, in my punch list, shown above, you can see after each item a 1, 2, up to a 5: Those are the number of times I wanted to hit that item.

How to Populate the Punch List

It probably won't surprise you, but I think that, when it comes to populating the punch list, the best information comes from looking at your scenes, your series, and your theme.

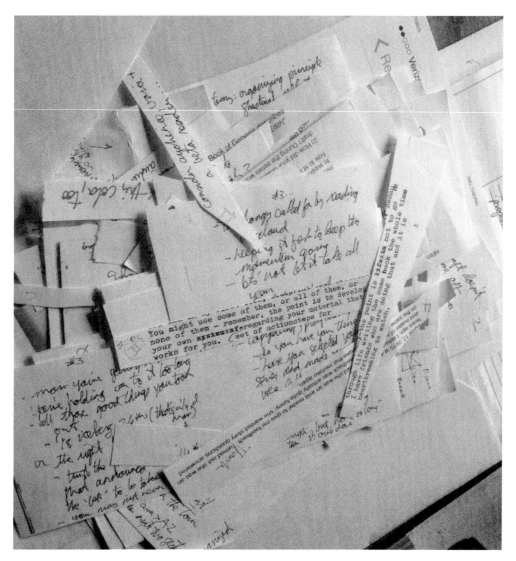

Does each of your scenes do its job? Is there a scene (or six) that you can just lift out of the manuscript? Any time something slides right out, and it's almost like no one notices it, you have to take that as a sign. As Ro$hi says, "Which of your bad and forgotten scenes are you going to rewrite, and which will you just discard?" Later, in the section about *Hemingway's Iceberg*, we will see that even if we remove them these scenes did not go to waste. And a good scene, one that we "made (even) better" during the second draft? It may not need one more single thing.

When considering your series, it helps if you have done "grid maintenance" while writing the second draft. The series grid shows you, quite visibly, the items that are missing from your manuscript that need to make it on to your punch list for the third draft. You can also add a necessary series at this point—why not? If you look at my item number twenty-two, you can see that I received feedback from my beta readers that writers (the readers of my book) would be champing at the bit to identify their series while they were reading, and that I should give them some guidance and some action steps to help them out. Good idea; I put that in five times, in what I think were the right places. Of course, other times I just wanted to put something in once. You don't want to ruin the joke.

And finally, by now you know your theme. It may not have struck you like a bolt of lightning; it might have been more like a reasoned choice. It may have changed more than a few times before you settled on the one that makes the most sense. You'll know this is your theme because it is exciting, what you need to write to. It's the theme that makes discarding some decent stuff the least painful. Items on your punch list may be designed to carve other stuff away from the most telling appearances of your theme, in order to bring out that theme further in bold relief. You might sneak in additional references to your theme, because remember—your readers are not going to pick up everything you put down. It never hurts to suffuse a scene with the one thing your book is about, to the degree appropriate and enticing.

Keeping the Publication Wolves at Bay

Once you have your punch list fully populated, you have completed your preparations for the polished draft. As much as possible while you're creating this third draft, you need to keep the publication wolves at bay. Daydreams about acceptance (and the converse, anxiety attacks about rejection) are not going to be able to help at this point. You have been responsible and done some test marketing with your beta readers—it's not like you have no idea what chords your book may be striking—but right now you need to finish this draft on its own terms. There may be compelling publication-related reasons to complete a draft after this, such as collaboration with a literary agent or submission to a publisher, but we are bracketing all of that for now. Right now we have our audience in mind, and we are using the voice that we think will reach them, and everything else will have to wait.

Why Some People Don't Finish

This is kind of a heavy topic, but since it is related to what we just discussed I think I'll bring it up now. Obviously, I think that a lot of the reasons people don't finish is because they don't have a structured process to know what they need to be working on, when. That's a pretty innocent way of getting lost that hopefully this book has helped a little with. Some people don't finish because they can't keep the publication wolves at bay, the pressure from the outside world gets too intense, or they can't bring themselves to put themselves out there as the author of this book. They may have what are called *hidden, related commitments*—something just as strong or stronger that is working against them being a successful, published author.

Whether you want to get really deep about it, or just say, "I can't seem to find the time..." there is one thing I want to say that will seem pretty obvious. The people who quit, can't make it. If you look at the subset circle of people who didn't make it, the entire subset of people who quit is contained within that. Finishing requires tenacity. Taking something all the way to the end always looks kind of insane. Of course, it won't feel insane. It will feel indescribably satisfying.

Hemingway's Theory of the Iceberg

When you look at your punch list, you may find that some of the items indicate things you want to remove. Scenes that are flat or uninteresting because they aren't animated by any series, series that don't relate to the theme, everything related to that second theme that is nestled inside your manuscript like an enemy inside a Trojan horse—all of that will have to go.

You have to trust the process, the same one that said to raise the best parts up a level. Those other parts, that weren't the best parts—you don't need them. Or rather, you don't need them anymore. It might be difficult to part with those pieces that started a fire somewhere inside of you, and led to other discoveries that were closer and closer to the heart of the matter.

If it makes you feel any better, Ernest Hemingway thought you should take out seven-eighths of what you know about a subject; the top one-eighth is the tip of the iceberg, what the reader reads. The catch is, the reader knows if you don't know the other seven-eighths. Then they feel that your writing is not solid or substantive enough to enjoy, but rather just an ice floe on the loose.

Hemingway's Theory of the Iceberg is also called the *theory of omission*. Hemingway even went so far as to believe that the quality of a piece could be judged by the quality of the material the author eliminated.[7]

• • • • • • • • • • • •

7   Jeffrey Meyers, *Hemingway: A Biography* (Boston: Da Capo Press, 1999), 139.

That may mess with your target word count in a particular genre, but it's more likely to mess with your faith. Can something really be gone and still be here at the same time?

I've seen it. I recently took a 3,000-word essay down to 1,700 words, while also adding some new material (always an option in the polished draft). I read it the other day, and I didn't actively miss any of the good stuff that hit the cutting-room floor. What was there was everything I wanted to say.

Write That Polished Draft!

When the time comes to write the polished draft, I recommend hopping around the manuscript. The first draft you did in whatever order it came to you. The second draft you definitely want to write straight through, as you use your series to change stuff around.

But in the third draft you can go anywhere the day is calling. On my punch list you can see I highlighted the items I wanted to work on during a certain session and then crossed off what I had accomplished. It was probably human nature that I went after the easiest things first.

Hopping around helps you to avoid getting bogged down in all of the decisions that have been made to this point in a part that's finished anyway. It relieves you of the (false) obligation to examine everything anew. Sometimes I say, "If it doesn't need it, you won't get it." That makes sense, right? When you study a paragraph that is done, nothing happens.

So why waste your time? By now you have enough of a feel for the whole to go where there is work to be done. You know the emotional tenor of this scene; you know the information the reader has at this point. The more closely you can focus on what actually needs to change, the more energy you can bring to the real questions on the table. The opposite of this is going through every page in the book looking to vaguely improve it. That's not much of a mandate. The best way to keep the momentum is to keep the subject matter of your revision fresh. Or, as one of the mantras for this draft might read: "Hit it, and get out."

Here are a few more mantras to keep you company while you create your polished draft:

* *what's done is done*
* *when in doubt, take it out*
* *shortening the time spent on each draft helps you hold the whole thing in mind*
* *where does the work lie?*
* *make decisions*
* *stick to the strength of what has worked*
* *culminate*
* *keep it crisp*
* *heed the click*
* *don't lose heart*
* *trust yourself*
* *put it all together*
* *tighten the weave*
* *you could go on, but you don't need to, and in fact it's better if you don't*

The Crack in Everything

I n the messy draft, you likely experimented with a few different tones of voice until you figured out who your audience members were, and what tone of voice would reach them. In the method draft, you probably weren't able to help yourself from fiddling with perfectly good sentences to make them even better—even though you were supposed to be focusing on the "one thing your book is about." In the polished draft, you considered the individual words even more carefully. Using the right word, the one that you can pull off, is important. I just learned the word *compassion* like last week, for example, what it means.

But a word on wordsmithing: Sometimes when I work with clients, they ask me: "When are we going to talk about the actual writing, you know?" By that, they mean improving the vocabulary, or importing some metaphors, or redesigning the syntax. Part of me hopes the answer is: never. The idea that everything we've been doing thus far isn't writing, and that we're going to get to the writing, strikes me as a setup for pretension, or at the very least an overly complicated surface.

Are we wordsmithing to enhance our expression, or to make the writing bulletproof, somehow unassailable, and thereby protect ourselves? Sure, you can monkey around with it, you can read it aloud and change the placement of a comma to alter the reader's breath pattern in a sentence (without going all Oscar Wilde on it), you can add some subheads and change the title, but eventually you are going to have to stop.

You may have heard the story about Walt Whitman writing *Leaves of Grass*; in his best-known volume of poetry, he made up more words for the English language than anyone since Shakespeare. Words like describing the action of the wave against the shore as *slappy*, which is not a word, but was good enough to be.

As an old man, Whitman went back and did a lot of wordsmithing, taking out words like slappy and a hundred other bits of life—so much so that critics don't even use that later version. Or, if they do mention it, it is in an appendix in case you want to see someone screw up a work of art.[8]

You don't want to get to where you're holding on to your manuscript too long. One of my mentors in Prague, Jim Freeman, used to praise:

That fresh feeling,
of not having been too well-worked

· · · · · · · · · · · ·

8   For example, in line 54, Whitman replaced "slappy shore and laughs" with "shore where she laughs." *The Complete Writings of Walt Whitman*. Ed.s, Richard Maurice Bucke, Thomas Biggs Harned, Horace Traubel, Oscar Lovell Triggs (New York, G. P. Putnam's Sons, 1902).

The point is not to go through life writing the same book the whole time, remember. I have friends who are doing that and it is heartbreaking to watch.

Is anything made by human beings ever perfect? I'm a big fan of percentages, so let's say a book is 96% done; the effort to get it to 97% may cause you to run into some diminishing returns.

I could throw more metaphors at you here. If you've ever run a marathon, you know that the distance between mile 24 and mile 25 is not a mile. It is some godforsaken experience that is like no mile you've ever run before. During the writing of this book, the baseball pitcher Max Scherzer took a perfect game—no hits, no runs, no errors, no opposing player reaching base at all—into the ninth inning with two outs, and then he lost the perfect game by accidentally hitting somebody.

As the songwriter Leonard Cohen says, "There is a crack in everything / That's how the light gets in." I come from Philadelphia, so I can relate, since the symbol of the city that is on *everything* is a giant bell with a crack slashing diagonally across it.

You may just never nail Chapter Twenty-One. Questions about your work have percolated throughout this three-draft process. Some were answered early; some turned out to not be questions after all. Some benefited from input from your beta readers—and a few you may not have the answer to yet. What now, wait? Or roll with it?

I say roll with it because, ideally, you want to time finishing your final draft with the feeling of not wanting to work on it any more. While I was putting this book into a multimedia format, I made a good change to the text, but I made it in the version that was being sent off to be coded, and then there was a new version of those, and then I lost that tweak forever.

Some reader may find the error that I was correcting; it's happened before. In my first book, *BYB*, I was describing "making the time," which we also discussed in chapter one of this book. I advocated designing your own schedule—maybe you start writing at 4:45 a.m., or maybe you start writing at 9:00 p.m., go until 2:00 a.m., and then grab four hours of sleep, wake up, do your household duties, and then go back to sleep.

Why not? I quoted Keith Richards (because you can't always quote Saul Bellow), who said that the whole 9-to-5 thing is a remnant of the Industrial Revolution, which also gave us the notion of three square meals a day. Keith said we should free ourselves from those restrictions and that "when the hooter goes, you eat." (I noted that hooter is slang for nose.)

Cool, right? Yeah, until Nancy sent me an email:

Hi Stuart,
Just started reading your 'Blueprint' book, and your annotation
of the Keith Richard [sic] quote re our programmed eating
habits jumped off the page at me—indeed, 'hooter' is slang
for nose (if you're English—we Scots call it your 'neb'), but I
guess Keith didn't mean it in that sense. He surely meant the

hooter, or siren, klaxon, whatever you want to call it, which was sounded in factories to denote breaks in the day, like lunchtime? Looking forward to getting into the book anyway!

So basically, she was telling me, you're completely wrong. I think it's a small point. I think you should still buy the book. But I'm just saying that that kind of thing can't be avoided 100% of the time, so let's not pretend it can.

In my second book, *BA*, I couldn't figure out the exact relationship between a work that had multiple timelines and the concept of series; sometimes they acted the same, and sometimes they acted differently, like a photon of light that is both wave and particle. I have no idea what I'm talking about, and that is exactly my point. I did the best I could and I left it.

It is time to move on and tackle your next writing project. It's okay to admit you will miss the one you've just completed. It's always sad to say good-bye. But I would guess you have plans for taking this book out into the world where it will be right by your side for some time to come.

[Watch Video Nine: Biz Back to the City]

BIZ: DO I HAVE TO LEAVE? I MEAN, I WANT TO LEAVE, IS THAT WRONG?

I KNOW I'VE ALREADY ASKED THIS BUT, CAN'T YOU COME DOWN THE MOUNTAIN WITH ME?

RO$HI: I CAN COME FOR A LITTLE BIT.

BIZ: I WONDER WHAT IT'S GOING TO BE LIKE? ARE PEOPLE GOING TO LIKE MY BOOK?

BIZ: I KNOW NOT EVERYBODY'S GOING TO LIKE MY BOOK.

BIZ: BUT SOME PEOPLE WILL. AND I GUESS THAT'S MY AUDIENCE, RIGHT?

BIZ: I WAS GOING TO ASK YOU IF I CAN COME VISIT AGAIN SOME TIME, BUT YOU HAVEN'T BEEN ANSWERING A LOT OF MY QUESTIONS. LIKE, WHAT ARE YOU DOING HERE RIGHT NOW?

RO$HI: I HAVE TO PICK UP MY DRY-CLEANING.

BIZ: WELL CAN I
COME BACK? COULD
YOU STILL BE A
NEUTRAL AUDIENCE?

RO$HI: YOU DON'T NEED ME
ANY MORE. BESIDES,
NOW YOU HAVE THESE:

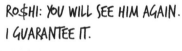

BIZ: WELL, WHAT ABOUT THE WHITE OX? WILL I EVER SEE HIM AGAIN? I KIND OF MISS HIS SWEET, TERRIFYING FACE.

RO$HI: YOU WILL SEE HIM AGAIN. I GUARANTEE IT.

THE END

Acknowledgments

The author wishes to thank...

...Dave Stebenne, video producer, storyboard creator, and voice of the White Ox, for his creativity and camaraderie throughout the whole process of watching something grow and continue to grow, while we followed it, and didn't get freaked out.

...Chloe Marsala, the voice of Biz—that some people may find ditzy, but then she did hike through Asia by herself and kept her personal power/wits about her to complete the entire journey.

...Beth Andrix Monaghan, my writing partner and unsung hero of this book, who asked all of the key questions and got all of the best jokes.

...Windy Lynn Harris, for being a transparently subjective beta reader and solar-powered source of joy.

...C.S. Plocher, who is about as versatile as a writing colleague can be; C.S. has started her own shop at csplocher.com—if you need what she's offering, you're in luck.

...Michele DeFilippo and Ronda Rawlins of 1106 Design, who are the answer to the trivia question: With whom can 72 emails about a project never get irritating?

...Molly Regan, of Logica Design, for her trademark vision, ridiculously short response times, and sly sense of humor while creating the covers and select interior graphics.

...Louann Pope, who turned the copy editing experience into a dialogue on music and strategy. Hire her at louannpope.com.

...Elisabeth Kauffman, of writingrefinery.com, for hopping on board the pencil train bound for glory with an informed proofread and supplemental copyedit embodying the genuine excitement of a fellow writer.

...Rob Degnan and Tim Ison, the rhythm section of Art Don't Pay, for the videos' "snazzy background music."

...Jenn Salcido, not just for allowing me to trot her theme out *yet again*, but for her supplemental proofread and identifying jokes that... weren't that funny.

...Andrew Boardman, Gina Bolvin, Tina Cassidy, Jane Friedman, Ashley Ghere, Pat Gifford, Vanessa Zuisei Goddard, Kimberly Hatfield, Claudia Horwitz, Don Lafferty, Rich Markow, Julie Matheson, Tom Matlack, Nancy McKnight, Susan Pohlman, Whitney Scharer, Paula Spiese, Lynn Wiese Sneyd, Jeanette Stokes, Jessica Strawser, and Liza Ward for their contributions to what is at heart a team effort.

...the organizations that have hosted me across the country where so much of the best material was developed: Book Passage, Clarksville Writer's Conference, Crested Butte Writer's Conference, Falmouth Public Library, InkHouse Public Relations, Palm Springs Writer's Group, Pennwriters Conference, Philadelphia Writer's Conference, Pikes Peak Writers, Redwood Writers, Resource Center for Women & Ministry in the South, Rocky Mountain Fiction Writer's Conference, San Francisco Writer's Conference, San Diego State Writer's Conference, Tucson Festival of Books, Wellesley Books, Wheatmark, The Writer, and Writer's Digest.

...and finally, my three peas in a pod: Bonnie, Fifer, and Bodhi, who make life worth living every single day.

STUART HORWITZ is a ghostwriter, independent developmental editor, and the founder and principal of Book Architecture (www. BookArchitecture.com).

He developed the Book Architecture Method over fifteen years of helping writers get from first draft to final draft. In the process, those same writers have become authors: signing with top literary agencies, landing book deals at coveted publishing houses, and pursuing successful paths to independent publishing.

Book Architecture's clients have reached the *New York Times*-bestseller lists in both fiction and nonfiction, and have appeared on *The Oprah Winfrey Show, Today, The Tonight Show*, and in the most prestigious journals in their respective fields.

Horwitz's first book, *Blueprint Your Bestseller: Organize and Revise Any Manuscript with the Book Architecture Method* (Penguin/Perigee) was named one of the best books about writing by The Writer magazine. His second book, *Book Architecture: How to Plot and Outline Without Using a Formula* was released in 2015 as part of a five-year, 100-venue book tour of North America that will run through 2017.

Horwitz holds degrees in literary aesthetics from New York University and East Asian studies from Harvard University. He is also an award-winning poet and essayist.

He lives in Rhode Island with his wife and two daughters.